Foundations of Discipleship

Foundations of Discipleship

Patrick Gahan

ISBN 978-0-557-41454-3

To my mother, who provided the foundation for my faith.

Introduction

This book came about due to a challenge from my wife. Some years ago when we were serving in Maryland and I was preparing for an adult Confirmation class, I shared with Kay the book I planned to use in that class. She spent a few hours studying it, and then looked me square in the face, "Pat, you could read this entire book and still not know what it means to be a Christian, and you certainly would not have the foggiest idea of how to live as one." I started writing the very next day!

My wife's was not the only voice that cajoled me into action. About that same time, I read the words of Yale theologian Miroslav Volf: *Pastors can mediate faith as a way of life only if they find it compelling themselves and if their parishioners are moved by it because it makes sense of their lives.*[1]

On that accord, this book not only offers a window into our shared Christian faith but one into my personal walk, as well. I do hope you will be moved by my words and join me in the most marvelous journey of all – that of a lifelong, devoted disciple of Jesus Christ.

Patrick Gahan+
Epiphany, 2010

---

[1] Miroslav Volf, "Way of Life," <u>The Christian Century</u> (Nov. 20, 2002)

Contents

Chapter 1

What is a Life of Faith?

What is faith?

Once I was paid to fall. It was my job. Surrounded by 90 others, I would rise at 6:00 AM each day, run five miles, do scores of pushups, countless pull-ups, and all day practice falling into huge circus rings of sawdust.

We began falling off of platforms no higher than a curb on a neighborhood street. By the time our training was over, we were falling from 250 ft. towers. The falls were called *PLFs* – Parachute Landing Falls. Once we mastered the fine art of falling, they flew us up into the heavens in dark green aircraft, and we fell through metal doors towards farmlands that suddenly looked like postage stamps and trees that looked like pipe cleaners.

The U.S. Army paid us to fall, and they wanted us to fall correctly so we could fall again the next day. When we would fall out those doors hurtling toward the gray smoke marking the *LZ* – the Landing Zone, we would count "one thousand, two thousand, three thousand, four thousand," and then look up to see if the static line had worked and we had a canopy above us.

We spent over 120 hours just learning how to fall. The message was simple really, turn your parachute into the wind, curl your body sideways like a parenthesis, and hit the ground with the fleshy parts of your body. What the Army could have taught us in an afternoon, they extended over three arduous weeks of numerous five-mile runs, scores of pushups, multitudinous pull-ups, and punctuated with innumerable falls into the dusty sawdust pit. They wanted us to know how to fall, so for three weeks we lived in the sawdust pits. I have not fallen out of an aircraft in 23 years, but I still recall every element of my instruction. Because my life, like yours, is full of falls, I have never quit wishing that the whole earth was covered in sawdust, and rarely have I forgotten to look up.

Faith is about falling and knowing. In an odd sort of way, the life of faith can be compared to a soldier jumping out of the side door of a C-130 transport plane. Each time you jump you feel the fear and realize the risk of so great a fall. Somewhere on the more solid ground of the psyche is the knowledge that you are connected to that big aircraft by a braided nylon static line, and because you are connected, you believe the parachute will open making your fall no more calamitous than the first ones you completed in the big circles of sawdust.

An initial step into the Christian life is to admit that people fall – to admit that each one of us falls again and again. Sometimes we fall due to poor personal choices, sometimes we fall due to heartbreak, and other times we fall because our world cracks open for seemingly no reason at all and we no longer have a place to stand. Christians fall like other people, yet we do so knowing that we are connected to One much greater than us, our circumstance, or even our world.

It is a misrepresentation of the Christian life to imagine it to be one free of discord and disappointment, an escape from the raging ocean of life into some placid inland pond. The fact that the one we call Lord, Jesus Christ, entered into the human situation complete with its trials, blood, guts, and death should tell us differently. In what was likely the very first Christian song, the apostle Paul not only admits but also celebrates this central tenet of the Christian life.

Philippians 2:5-11 (NRSV)

5 Let the same mind be in you that was in Christ Jesus,
6 who, though he was in the form of God,
did not regard equality with God
as something to be exploited,
7 but emptied himself,

taking the form of a slave,
being born in human likeness.
And being found in human form,
8 he humbled himself
and became obedient to the point of death—
even death on a cross.
9 Therefore God also highly exalted him
and gave him the name
that is above every name,
10 so that at the name of Jesus
every knee should bend,
in heaven and on earth and under the earth,
11 and every tongue should confess
that Jesus Christ is Lord,
to the glory of God the Father.

In a very tangible sense, these ancient lyrics state that Christians fall because Jesus Christ, the one we call *Lord*, has fallen himself. He who was and is God chose to become a human and take the worst life can dole out. The song reminds us that there is nothing escapist about the Christian life. If anything, Christians, like their Lord, embrace all of life, both the sweet and the bitter.

The antithesis of a life that embraces not only the joy but the suffering of human existence is the one painted by Aldous Huxley in Brave New World. In that futuristic world Huxley imagined, so close to our grasp now, there is no pain in death because the dying are placed in antiseptic hospital rooms and tranquilized for the final portion of death's journey, much like the euthanasia we impose on a family pet. However, in order to tame death in that futuristic state, human relationships such as marriage and parenting have been terminated. To conquer the sting of death and pain, the sources of pain must be abolished – commitment, empathy, and love. In Huxley's world, the pain of final death has been replaced by a walking death. It is a life without destination.

Christian faith, however, is rooted in the knowledge that human life is going somewhere. In other words, even though our lives individually and collectively are fraught with falls of one sort or the other, we know our existence is far from pointless. Rather, it is full of meaning. After all, the great comedy of the New Testament is that every shred of evidence shouted that Jesus' life was a miserable failure (I use *comedy* here in the dramatic sense). The cross was the exclamation point on a revolution gone bust with Jesus himself as the defeated, dying clown. Yet the joke was on the Romans and the religious bureaucrats who murdered him. There is not a single ancient song about Pontius Pilate's or Caiphas's victory. However, every day new songs are added to this first century one recounted by Paul and all of them rejoicing in the victory of Christ. We can have faith that our history is going somewhere because we are connected to Jesus, the fallen clown. Methodius, the third century bishop of Olympus, notes the new picture God paints of the human destination.

> *Being in the image of God, (humanity) still needed to receive the likeness. The Word (Jesus Christ), having been sent into the world to perfect this, first took on our own form, even though in history it has been stained by many sins, so that we for our part, on whose account he bore it, should be once again capable of partaking in his divine nature. Hence it is now possible for us to receive God's likeness. Think of a skilled painter painting a likeness of himself on a surface. So we may now imitate the same characteristics that God himself has displayed in becoming a human being. We hold onto these characteristics as we go in discipleship along the path he set out. His purpose in consenting to put on human flesh when he was God was this: that we, upon seeing the divine image in this tablet, so to speak, might imitate this incomparable artist.*[2]

---

[2] Methodius, Symposium 1.4.24., as cited in Ancient Christian Commentary on Scripture, Vol. VII, p.239

In a bizarre paradox of the Christian life, our many falls draw us closer to God rather than further. The crucified comedian falls first so that we might be tethered to him, the rock of our being and the master painter of a genuine life.

One of my wife's and my favorite restaurants has a catchy slogan printed on each one of its menus: "Life's short; eat dessert first." I must confess that the desserts in this restaurant are so delectable that my entrée is merely an extended preamble to the Chocolate Decadence Cake or some other rich fare they are offering that day. I may be eating chicken salad on a croissant, but I am thinking chocolate cake on my fork. Christian faith looks forward to the dessert of life. I do not mean that Christians believe in *Pie in the sky by and by*, that we are in some sort of a grin and bear it holding pattern until we die. No, I mean exactly the opposite. We can extend ourselves fully into this life, squeezing out every ounce of what the present offers, because we know our story's conclusion. We have trust that our lives are comedy and not tragedy because we look forward to the final course before it has been served.

John of Patmos, the author of the last book of the Bible – Revelation, reflects on the end of our story in a way that has challenged Christians for two thousand years. John's world along with his life has taken a terrible fall. Whether due to direct Roman imperial persecution or persecution of a more subtle nature, John and his Christian colleagues are under oppressive judgment by the state and thereby have been relegated to the margins of their culture. While John is in this free-fall from stability, he is given a concurrent vision illuminating his own world with visions of the heavenly court. On the surface, what looks like arbitrary meanness and brutality against a gentle people takes on unconquerable meaning when viewed from the exalted court of Christ, the crucified Lamb of God. Therefore, for most of Revelation's twenty-two chapters, John has his feet in two places – on earth and in heaven. John's vision rolls to a climatic conclusion in chapter 21.

Revelation 21:1-6 (NRSV)

*1 Then I saw a new heaven and a new earth; for the first
heaven and the first earth had passed away, and the sea
was no more.2 And I saw the holy city, the new
Jerusalem, coming down out of heaven from God,
prepared as a bride adorned for her husband.3 And I
heard a loud voice from the throne saying,
"See, the home of God is among mortals.
He will dwell with them as their God;
they will be his peoples,
and God himself will be with them;
4 he will wipe every tear from their eyes.
Death will be no more;
mourning and crying and pain will be no more,
for the first things have passed away."
5 And the one who was seated on the throne said, "See, I
am making all things new." Also he said, "Write this, for
these words are trustworthy and true."6 Then he said to
me, "It is done! I am the Alpha and the Omega, the
beginning and the end. To the thirsty I will give water as
a gift from the spring of the water of life.*

Like John, all Christians have their feet planted both on earth and in heaven. We are sojourners here continually on a journey to God. Early Christians, as a matter of fact, during those periods of imperial persecution would often give "Jerusalem" as their home of origin, in effect their permanent address. The response would bewilder their Roman captors. While they had been terribly diminished in their present culture, their ultimate destination was completely out of the grasp of their temporal adversaries. Hence, those early Christians were free to live in whatever state they found themselves. Much later, the twentieth century author C.S. Lewis noted that Christians are "amphibious," living in two realms at the very same time. We, like Lewis and our ancient brothers and sisters, know our life is going somewhere, and all the pain and distress heaped onto us by the world will not impede our sweet journey.

Pierre Teilhard De Chardin, the esteemed Jesuit scientist and theologian, said it is a mistake to think that we are "human beings having a spiritual experience." No, he said, "we are spiritual beings having a human experience." Our faith is rooted in the certain knowledge that we are the divine intention of God and not some protoplasmic mistake. Our beginning is in God; therefore, our ending will be in God as well. Christ is the "Alpha and Omega" of those who have faith in him, and that is our "just desserts." Knowing the end or our story gives us the unassailable faith to live out our years with great courage, vitality, and joy. This is what Jesus means when he says to his followers, "I have come that you may have life and have it in all abundance." (John 10:10)

How do I deal with doubt?

I must be quick to admit that in the midst of our many and myriad falls and because of our ability to reason, it is easy to doubt the truth of our faith. Our ultimate origin and destination in God is hardly verifiable on this side of life. In a stroke of stark honesty, the writer of Hebrews admits the illusive quality of our faith: "Now faith is the assurance of things hoped for, the conviction of things not seen." (Hebrews 11:1) Jesus, on the other hand, admonishes his disciple Thomas for his need for tactile evidence in order to maintain his faith: "Have you believed because you have seen me? Blessed are those who have not seen and yet have come to believe." (John 20:29) As much as we like to poke fun at Thomas, he is simply expressing the thoughts that rise up in us from time to time. Regardless of what we have read in the Bible and what we have been taught by those who have shepherded us, both our fears and our reason lead us to doubt the veracity of our faith time and again.

Sigmund Freud, the father of psychoanalysis, was so compelled by the scant empirical evidence of religious faith and the fear he imagined motivating it that he wrote <u>The Future of an Illusion</u> in order to disprove Jewish and Christian faith. In that work, Freud persuasively states that our faith in God is nothing more than wishful thinking. To Freud, faith is simply a projection of our need for a divine father, a larger-than-life being who will take care of us. Our psyche's defense against the procession of falls that occur to humanity is the false construction of a cosmic band-aid.

While those words sound harsh to the Christian, Freud has actually done us a great service. It is a mistake to put our faith in a paternalistic caretaker God. Having faith that our beginnings and endings are in God is not a life without misfortune or a life that abandons rational thought, but it is a life laden with ultimate meaning. One of the oldest stories in the Bible is the lengthy epic poem Job. The protagonist, Job, is furious with God because he has experienced cataclysmic falls, even though he is noted as a most righteous man. Job, nevertheless, has lost the people and things most dear to him through a series of catastrophes. Furthermore, four associates who come to soothe him do nothing but rub salt in his wounds by asserting that Job has no doubt received what he deserved from God. When Job has had a belly full of his friends' poorly informed comments and the seemingly random and capricious treatment he has received from God, he raises his own voice in protest.

Job 10:18-22 (NRSV)

18 "Why did you bring me forth from the womb?
Would that I had died before any eye had seen me,
19 and were as though I had not been,
carried from the womb to the grave.
20 Are not the days of my life few?
Let me alone, that I may find a little comfort
21 before I go, never to return,
to the land of gloom and deep darkness,
22 the land of gloom and chaos,
where light is like darkness."

While Job still retains enough belief in God to raise his fist at him, he no longer sees the meaning of human creation. He does not believe his own life is going anywhere. He certainly does not understand why any God worth believing in would allow these bad things to occur to him. God's response comes thundering back. Laced with sarcasm, God wants to know who appointed Job the master of life and death.

Job 38:4-7 (NRSV)

4 "Where were you when I laid the foundation of the earth?
Tell me, if you have understanding.
5 Who determined its measurements—surely you know!
Or who stretched the line upon it?
6 On what were its bases sunk,
or who laid its cornerstone
7 when the morning stars sang together
and all the heavenly beings shouted for joy?

Perhaps that is why Job is every person. It is easy enough to retain faith that something beyond us began the great process of creation, but we may not see any purpose behind our lives. In fact, more often than not, it seems the divine only bursts into our lives with pain and travail. In truth, our encounters with God are not always warm and paternal. On occasion, they are awesome and even fearful. Beginning and ending with God does not mean a journey with an equal – far from it. Our very subordinate position in the presence of the Creator is intensified in those encounters. The modern social critic Christopher Lasch asserts in opposition to Freud that the God of scripture is not a "God of personal convenience."[3] Instead the mighty God of Job and Revelation is One who demands something from humans because we were divinely knit to participate in God. Our lives are going somewhere, but we need to take a large dose of humility and give up the illusion of being our own *alpha and omega* in order to discern our direction.

---

[3] Christopher Lasch, "The Illusion of Disillusionment," Harpers, July 1991, pp. 19-22

The real hope of Christian faith is set on the rock of a future in God. However, the strength of this developing faith is incubated in the house of memory. My initial remembered encounters with God illustrate this point. While I may sound presumptuous attributing these early adolescent encounters to God, my fuzzy Sunday School notions of faith were toppled by these engagements. The God who would inculcate my singular unimpressive life into divine history became both a fearful and awesome God to me during these almost routine encounters. Rudolph Otto, the markedly influential German writer, asserts in his book <u>The Idea of the Holy</u> that our meetings with God are punctuated with both the allure of fascination and the dread of fear – both experienced simultaneously. Shortly after World War I, Otto wrote: "Just as 'wrath', taken in a purely rational or a purely ethical sense, does not exhaust that profound *awefulness* (his italics) which is locked in the mystery of the deity, so neither does 'graciousness' exhaust the profound element of *wonderfulness* and rapture which lies in the mysterious beatific experience of deity."[4] To meet up with God is to be changed. The God who enters human history as Jesus Christ and offers himself to be crucified by the very people he loved and desired to save is anything but domesticated.

As a young teen, I served as the Sunday Sexton (janitor) of the local Episcopal parish. The church house was always dark when I would arrive at 5:30 AM. I would walk down the long, red-carpeted aisle in respectful awe of what I might find there. Occasionally a hobo would suddenly rise up in the pew before my face like a resurrected corpse and then casually ask me what time it was or when the coffee would be made, a dog who had found his way onto the soft carpet of the nave would silently come up behind me and greet me with an unexpected lick of my hand, or a trapped bird would fly fiercely across the vaulted ceiling of the chancel with the flutter of a ghostly apparition. These were the last days of unlocked sanctuaries in the city. It was my job to turn on the lights, sweep the entrance and the sidewalks, and turn on the large coffee urn before the early service

---

[4] Rudolf Otto, trans. John W. Harvey, <u>The Idea of the Holy</u> (London: Oxford University Press, 1923), 32.

commenced at All Saint's Church in Birmingham, AL. From time to time I had company, yet they would leave as the sleepy-eyed communicants slipped silently into their familiar pews and onto their knees in preparation for the 7:30 Holy Communion.

I was thirteen, and that unlit, long, carpeted aisle was my first remembered journey toward God. In truth, I feared the hoboes, dogs, and birds far less than I did the God who inhabited that still dark sanctuary.

Later on Sunday mornings, as I was setting up Sunday School Rooms in the undercroft, I would hear the customary canticles of Morning Prayer rolling disturbingly down the stairs to me.

> For the Lord is a great God and a great King above all gods.
> In his hand are all the corners of the earth,
> And the heights of the hills are his also.
> O come let us worship and fall down
> And kneel before the Lord our Maker...

And the Benedictus would echo closely behind the heels of the Venite. (The Venite is taken from Psalms 95 and 96; the Benedictus is taken from *The Song of Three Young Men* found in Apocrypha.)

> Blessed art thou that beholdest the depths,
> And dwellest between the Cherubim;
> Praised and exalted above all forever.

The God I encountered there was no chum. To fall into his grasp was serious business. And these feelings of awe were only confirmed later when I was sent to St. Andrew's School at age fourteen. There amongst the mountains of the Cumberland Plateau in Tennessee the Holy Cross monks carried a Bible in one hand and a board in the other and felt that time boys spent on their knees was never wasted. Our daily retreat into the musty, stuccoed chapel, whose landscape was dominated by the wood-hewn, life-sized crucifix centered on the north wall, was a sojourn into that other world. Elizabethan English mingled with Medieval Latin, incense so thick the altar appeared to be floating, and the chilling, crisp ring of the Sanctus bells reverberated through our ears disturbing our adolescent apathy with something akin to quixotic urgency.

> *Holy, Holy, Holy, Lord God of Hosts:*
> *Heaven and earth are full of thy glory.*
> *Glory be to thee, O Lord Most High.* (Isaiah 6)

I would have scoffed at the suggestion that I was religious during my teenaged years. I can only remember electively praying before basketball games, trigonometry tests, and dateless Saturday nights. But I was not quarantined from the spiritual world. What's more, I was spared empty, pietistic notions of a god who was fashioned much more like a kindly great uncle than the One who dwells between the winged Cherubim and holds the very corners of the earth in his hand. I learned he was a jealous God, a "consuming fire," that he wanted all or nothing, and that yellowing, tormented Christ on the chapel's north wall was testimony to just how serious God was. This was told to me by men and women, who, for no apparent reason, taught, pushed, coached, chided, nudged, and urged me and a host of other hapless boys through our secondary education as if we had some intrinsic worth and our lives were going somewhere. God knows that was news to most of us.

Those Anglican canticles, Gregorian chants, papery wafers, and sweet port wine remained deep within me long after I exited the doors of All Saints' Church and the gates of St. Andrew's School and so did the adults who knelt beside me in those padless pews. That does not mean I did not want to run from God. I did, and I have done so time and again. But the seeds of my conversion were planted deep within the soil of my self. I cannot boast, therefore, of my decision to seek God and remain on this journey. Ultimately, I have learned that Otto was right – God is fearfully irresistible.

What will faith require of me?

This fearful, yet irresistible experience of God is our complement to faith's doubt. I say complement and not antidote, for the latter would suppose Christian doubt could be extinguished. It cannot. Paul Tillich, the philosopher-theologian who escaped from Nazi Germany to America, stated that doubt is an ingredient of faith. Tillich had witnessed a whole country, a noble way of life, fall into consummate evil. Faith without doubt would be a charade to him or to anyone coming out of such a deadly experience. Accordingly, Tillich acknowledged that faith is risky business. A person steps out in faith to follow the God of Job and John uncertain if the journey will lead to fulfillment in God but "betting the farm" that it does.

Fear, fascination, doubt, and risk are all aspects of Christian faith we should remember as we begin the journey. Those elements would be lessened if faith was merely a matter of looking deep within our self, taking an inventory of our useful gifts, godly traits, and overall goodness, and then making plans for a life congruent with our personal abilities and decency factors. But the journey embarks from God – not from us. The notion of "making something out of your self" is not a Christian formula. God, the fearful, fascinating Other will make something out of each one of us. God will make us someone. That is why faith is risky business. It is not defined or controlled by humanity.

Paul, in his most comprehensive theological work, his Letter to the Romans, sets up his exposition of faith by using the example of the Jewish patriarch Abraham. At the onset of his argument, Paul denies that Abraham had any exemplary qualities or a godliness quotient that made him particularly attractive for God's service. The evidence from the Old Testament supports Paul's claim. Essentially, Abraham is as human as any other personality in the Bible, which makes him as prone to falls as the rest of us. Paul states that Abraham's courage to risk it all on an obscure call and promise from an unknown God is what distinguishes him and thereby makes him the "father" of Christian faith.

Romans 4:16-24 (The Message)

For Abraham is father of us all. He is not our racial father—that's reading the story backwards. He is our faith father. We call Abraham "father" not because he got

God's attention by living like a saint, but because God made something out of Abraham when he was a nobody. Isn't that what we've always read in Scripture, God saying to Abraham, "I set you up as father of many peoples"? Abraham was first named "father" and then became a father because he dared to trust God to do what only God could do: raise the dead to life, with a word make something out of nothing. When everything was hopeless, Abraham believed anyway, deciding to live not on the basis of what he saw he couldn't do but on what God said he would do. And so he was made father of a multitude of peoples. God himself said to him, "You're going to have a big family, Abraham!" Abraham didn't focus on his own impotence and say, "It's hopeless. This hundred-year-old body could never father a child." Nor did he survey Sarah's decades of infertility and give up. He didn't tiptoe around God's promise asking cautiously skeptical questions. He plunged into the promise and came up strong, ready for God, sure that God would make good on what he had said. That's why it is said, "Abraham was declared fit before God by trusting God to set him right." But it's not just Abraham; it's also us! The same thing gets said about us when we embrace and believe the One who brought Jesus to life when the conditions were equally hopeless.

Paul uses Abraham as the model of our faith because in his story is evidence that faith begins and ends with God. We may think we are "hopeless" and of no use to God, or we may imagine that our situation is "hopeless" and un-redeemable by God. On both counts we have departed the faith of Abraham and made a god of ourselves. Furthermore, because God is the inaugurator of faith, everything is required of us to meet the demand. Perhaps the riskiest aspect of the Christian faith is that humans do not define its contents or its demand. The life of faith is awesome for an awesome, unmanageable God determines it. Tillich made another assertion in this matter that I like very much as well. He declared that faith requires the entire person. We do not risk certain parts of our self. No, we put the entire self, warts and all, into the service of God. To hold back unseemly parts or to sequester parts of our life as out-of-bounds and unavailable to God is playing at faith, not living it.

Recently, a friend of mine made a disturbing comment in one of her sermons. She said, "Because we receive the gospel in comfort, we must resist the temptation to construct a Gospel of comfort." She, of course, was observing that modern Americans are not persecuted on account of their faith. The temptation for us then is to adulterate faith into something it is not. It is to remake the Christian life into Freud's caricature, a faith built upon human demand and personal actualization. The world rejoices in such a tame, toothless faith, for it has no power to change lives or circumstance. Faith is not a pacifier. It is, instead, to be swept up into the life of God and given a life of purpose. Don't imagine that faith will offer you comfort any more than comfort was extended to Christ. Expect unfathomable love but not comfort.

Matthew 10:16-18 (The Message)

"When people realize it is the living God you are presenting and not some idol that makes them feel good, they are going to turn on you, even people in your own family. There is a great irony here: proclaiming so much love, experiencing so much hate! But don't quit. Don't cave in. It is all well worth it in the end.

Discussion Questions for Chapter 1
What is a Life of Faith?

Our Stories

Remember a story about a turning point in your own life – religious, personal, professional, or otherwise.

Reading Review

1. Is faith in God just an *escape* route out of the harsh realities of life?

2. Does *doubt* have any place in the life of faith?

3. Why does faith always include an element of *risk* for us?

Bible Connections

1. Read **Isaiah 6:1-8**. Do you think Isaiah would flee this scene if he could? How does Isaiah describe a close encounter with God?

2. Read **Job 10:18-22**. How despondent is Job, and what is his dark wish? Have you felt like Job at some point in your life?

3. Read **Hebrews 11:1-2, 8-12**. Why does the author of Hebrews extol Abraham as his role model of faith? Do his reasons attract or repel you?

4. Read **Revelation 7:9-17**. The Bible story ends with a magnificent portrait of those who have led a life of faith and God's faithfulness to them. How would you restate in more modern terms what it means to "wash our robes in the blood of the lamb"?

Chapter 2

Why is Jesus Christ the Focus of Our Faith?

Does life have a purpose?

As a boy, I desperately wanted to be a workingman. The men I admired most were those who left the house everyday a little before sunrise, with a black lunch pail in one hand and a yellow hard hat held in the crook of their arm. I thought, and I still think, that there was something immensely noble about a man who worked hard with his hands all day and then returned home to a grateful family. I wanted to be counted in their number when I grew up, and I took every opportunity to work beside those men in various neighborhood projects that arose most weekends.

Therefore, it was no surprise to anyone when my redheaded next-door neighbor Corky Potter told me that his family was putting a new shingle roof on their house the next Saturday morning, I begged to help them with the work. Like a modern day Tom Sawyer, Corky tormented me with indecision before he begrudgingly agreed to let me work on their roof in the midst of Alabama's stifling July heat. Once he relented, however, the roofing job commencing next door had me so excited that I could hardly sleep the night before. I was sitting on the front curb for an hour before a single ladder was put up against the wood frame house.

My anticipation was fully rewarded. Mr. Potter and his two strapping nephews allowed me to work with them throughout the day. I carried precariously balanced fifty-pound packages of roofing materials up the ladder, nailed in asphalt shingles with a twelve-ounce hammer while clenching extra galvanized nails between my teeth, and glued in bright aluminum flashings with fiery hot, gooey, black tar. The day was so satisfying that I lost all track of time. It was not until Corky's mother yelled up the ladder that supper was ready and the smell of fried chicken wafted up to the roof from the kitchen window that I realized that I was ravenously hungry. I could already see myself seated around the table with the other tired, dirty, and sweaty "men" eating scores of golden chicken thighs, a mountain of chilled potato salad, and drinking gallons of sugary sweet iced tea. It would be the perfect ending to a perfect day for me.

Because I wanted to take one more look at our work of art atop my neighbor's house, I was the last one down the ladder. As I descended rung by rung over the dining room window, I heard Mrs. Potter say, "Corky, you can hand Pat a glass of iced tea to drink on the porch, but I do not want that white trash in my house." I was devastated. I can remember only sitting on the bottom back step of the Potter home unable to move with a plastic glass full of iced tea propped between my tar-splattered *Converse* tennis shoes. My mother looked out the door of our house and called me home. I walked through the door, fell into her arms, and began to sob. "Mama, they called me trash," was all I could say in the intervals of my heaving convulsions. When I had cried myself out, she held me at arm's length and said in her confident and stern manner, "Pat, you are not trash. They cannot tell you who you are."

I am quite certain that Mother's brevity had more to do with her raging anger at our neighbors than her attempt at profundity. Yet her words were profound for me that day and have been beyond that day. The person who knew me better than any other, assured me that I was not "trash" and others could not define me. Thus, I reasoned, if I was not cosmic garbage, I must have some purpose in this life. However, if other human beings could not define that purpose for me, who could? That question has been the central quest of my entire life, and I have come to realize it is the question behind most others for the majority of my fellow human beings.

Rest assured, there is a cacophony of voices out there attempting to define each person's purpose. The Potter's voices join the chorus of many others insisting they know why we are here on earth. Some of the voices say our purpose is to stay thin and youthful at all costs. Others contend we must grab every sensation and thrill we can before we get old and die. Still others imagine the meaning of life is wrapped up in acquiring the money we need to purchase the things we want and the power we desire.

None of these voices are new. The search for the "fountain of youth" is at least as old as the Spanish conquistadors. The ancient Greek Epicureans coined the creed, "Eat, drink, and be merry for tomorrow you may die." Our collective obsession with money and power is much older than King Midas. Unfortunately, most of the people who would define us do so in much subtler ways. For example, have you noticed how news commentators and government officials rarely call people "citizens," but instead term us "consumers?" Capitalism, our much-touted economic system, quietly defines humanity's central purpose as consuming. How's that for a glamorous purpose? It always makes me think of a cow in a field eating grass all day – everyday. Surely human beings amount to more than that.

While I do not wish to critique our system of trade and industry, I do object to being defined by economists, just as I object to being defined by glamour magazine editors or Hollywood personalities or government leaders, for that matter. I believe God made human beings and only God has the right to define our purpose. That's the subject of the very first story of the Bible, as told in the first three chapters of Genesis. The scripture asserts we human beings, unlike all other creatures, are made in the image of God so that we can join in the care of creation and enjoy lively fellowship with God and with each other. Our purpose has never been as neatly stated as in the *Westminster Shorter Catechism*: "Man's chief end is to glorify God, and to enjoy Him forever." The biblical story begins with the assertion that we are made like God to both work and play to the delight of God.

Genesis 1:26-28

26 Then God said, "Let us make humankind in our image, according to our likeness; and let them have dominion over the fish of the sea, and over the birds of the air, and over the cattle, and over all the wild animals of the earth, and over every creeping thing that creeps upon the earth." 27 So God created humankind in his image, in the image of God he created them; male and female he created them.

What incredible freedom we have been given! Neither the Potters, nor the magazines at the grocery store checkout line, nor powerful bureaucrats, nor anyone else can define us – only the One who made us. Everything we do, our relationships, our work, our education, even our various amusements are to be exercised in the light of God's presence and offered to His glory. We no longer have to guess why we fall in love, go to school, find a job, raise a family, or any of the actions that make up a life. We do them because we are formed of divine substance to live a divinely centered life. Our whole life, both private and corporate, is an offering back to God. Every ounce of our life was designed by God to be charged with meaning. In that essential knowledge is found not only our purpose but also the avenue to insuperable joy.

What has gone wrong?

But something has gone terribly wrong. We can look around our world or simply look inside ourselves to see that we have forgotten our lives were fashioned to reflect the Creator's glory, that everything from our social relationships to our professional endeavors to even our most intimate private lives are to be offered back to God. Yet when we climb down the ladder of our exalted illusions, we realize that humanity has badly missed the mark.

A journey I made not more than a handful of years ago illustrates this illusory conception of our lives we all carry for a time. I was invited to downtown Manhattan for a business meeting. As I was visiting in

Pennsylvania at the time, a friend of mine suggested we drive into New Jersey and take the ferry over to the city. A business meeting that seemed at the outset like sheer drudgery had taken on the guise of an adventure. It was a crisp, bright autumn day when we pulled into Hoboken, New Jersey to catch the ferry across the bay to New York. I had flown into New York several times, and I had surveyed the magnificence of the city from several thousand feet above. This was a very different kind of experience. We left the dull, aging edifices of Hoboken and headed toward glittering Battery Park. Like a childhood recollection of Oz or Camelot, downtown Manhattan seemed enchanted from that vantage point. Of course, the magic castle appearing off the bow of the ferry was the silver shimmering Trade Towers. I expected the Wizard or King Arthur to pop out at any moment to greet us.

Like most of us, it is hard for me to reconcile that glorious memory picture from the ones paraded across our TV screens beginning September 11, 2001. Even on film, it looked as if dust from the destruction was falling in clumps upon the workers. Part of our universal despair over the terror delivered that day was the ruin of the Emerald City of our collective psyche. The dust of our innocence was falling down around our shoulders.

We were shocked the morning of September 11, and we should have been. Then again, perhaps we should not have been. The twentieth century was the most violent in the history of the world. The new millennium is simply beginning where the last one left off. We cannot hold this problem at arm's length like Eve quaking in the Garden of Eden pleading "the snake made me do it," and Adam pointing to Eve insisting, "she is to blame."

Genesis 3:12-13

12 The man said, "The woman whom you gave to be with me, she gave me fruit from the tree, and I ate."
13 Then the LORD God said to the woman, "What is this that you have done?" The woman said, "The serpent tricked me, and I ate."

We have the smell of forbidden fruit on our own lips, and it smells an awful lot like death. I do not wish to exonerate the Taliban, the al-Quaeda network, or any of the many enterprises of terror. Their deeds will be listed alongside those of Hitler, Stalin, the slave traders, and the many cunning conspirators of systematic evil throughout the ages. Nevertheless, if we would have evil overthrown, we had best look inside sooner rather than later.

St. Paul says that when we dare look inside ourselves, we will see that our sin is simply a grotesque rerun of Adam and Eve's first disobedient, self-serving, deceitful acts. So now the world is replete with sin. The initial aroma of that alluring fruit has been replaced by the stench of decay and death. Paul states now "death reigns" like a despotic tyrant. Death, he says is the evidence that we live in a dynasty of sin. Because we have fallen ever deeper into sin, our existence has become a meaningless procession only headed towards death.

Note that the sin of which Paul speaks is not little foibles, follies, and faux pas. No, it is ontological – the sin of Adam is now so pervasive that it has made its way into the very fiber of our being.[5] Certainly we can see proof of that in the disastrous affairs of the world, and we can view it close at hand within our own society. Mostly, however, we experience it through our distorted personal lives. Paul believes sin has flourished to such an extent that it has altered the very structure of reality. Thus, we are no longer what we were created to be. Quite literally, we are in a "hell" of a mess!

Romans 5:12-14

12 Therefore, just as sin came into the world through one man, and death came through sin, and so death spread to all because all have sinned—13 sin was indeed in the world before the law, but sin is not reckoned when there is no law.14 Yet death exercised dominion from Adam to Moses,

---

[5] Paul J. Achtemeier, Romans (Louisville: John Knox Press, 1985) p.100.

even over those whose sins were not like the transgression of Adam, who is a type of the one who was to come.

Can we be healed?

Seeing that sin and its cousin death have a stranglehold on us, what do we do? Again, just as the world is quick to define us, it is full of prescriptions promising remedy for our universal illness. Most of the advice sounds strangely akin to those who would tell us our purpose. "We need a harder body," "We must set some goals for success," "We should get a shiny new SUV and get more out of our weekends" are just a sampling of the louder voices assailing us. Yet deep down, we know those things are band-aids at best. They will never heal us.

Challenged by this lethal knowledge, a reporter once asked two questions of the great British mystery writer and classicist Dorothy Sayers: "Why does everything we do go wrong?" and "What is the meaning of all this suffering." Sayers answered the two queries with only three words: "The Christian answer to the first is 'Sin,' and to the second, 'Christ crucified.'"[6]

Even ardent church-going Christians like to dance by the crucified Christ, preferring the more sensible Jesus of the parables or the pastoral healing Jesus or the victorious resurrected Jesus. All of those aspects of Jesus are immensely important to us. However, it is the proclamation of Christ crucified that makes us take an uncomfortable personal look inward. We sidestep the crucified Christ not because of the gruesome image his sagging, bleeding body portrays, but because it confronts us with the destructive sin we know lies just beneath our composed exteriors. Simply stated, Christ dies an agonizing death reserved for the most despicable criminals because we humans sin.

While we are the despicable ones, we are unable to help ourselves. We are guilty as charged, yet with no power to rescue ourselves from death and the deadly existence that precedes our demise. So God steps into our darkness and takes the full measure of what we have coming to us. Fleming Rutledge of New York restates Paul's message, "The darkness of the day of

---

[6] Dorothy Sayers, quoted in Philip G. Ryken, The Message of Salvation (Downers Grove, IL: Inter Varsity Press, 2001), p. 44.

his death corresponds to the darkness of the human heart. The more we enter into the meaning of Christ's death, the closer we see into our own precariously balanced inner lives...We look at ourselves with the Savior's eyes and he looks at us. He looks at us in the same way he looked at every human being that he encountered in his earthly life—with infinite sadness for our predicament, yet with unquenchable love and unflinching resolve to rescue us from certain condemnation and death—whatever it takes, wherever it leads, whatever the price."[7]

Romans 5:6-11

> 6 For while we were still weak, at the right time Christ died for the ungodly. 7 Indeed, rarely will anyone die for a righteous person—though perhaps for a good person someone might actually dare to die. 8 But God proves his love for us in that while we still were sinners Christ died for us. 9 Much more surely then, now that we have been justified by his blood, will we be saved through him from the wrath of God. 10 For if while we were enemies, we were reconciled to God through the death of his Son, much more surely, having been reconciled, will we be saved by his life. 11 But more than that, we even boast in God through our Lord Jesus Christ, through whom we have now received reconciliation.

Twenty years after my mother held me and listened to my retching sobs due to my painful exclusion from the Potter's dinner table, I found myself crying over the telephone lines to her. My adult problems were more complicated than my childhood ones, I thought. I was married by then, and Kay and I had three children. To provide for them, I had taken a more lucrative yet grueling job that required me to travel a great deal. I lamented to my mother that the stress was suffocating me and the time spent away from our young children was growing increasingly more painful for me. Then I went on to list the necessity of my job. I bewailed our mortgage

---

[7] Fleming Rutledge, <u>The Undoing of Death</u> (Grand Rapids, MI: 2002) as adapted in <u>The Christian Century</u>, Vol. 119, No. 5, February 27, 2002, p.11.

payments, car notes, day care tuitions, and sundry other obligations. Mother listened to my litany attentively, and I fully expected her to respond with sympathy. Instead, she tersely answered my complaint with, "Son, you are only trapped if you think you are."

I was so enraged by what I thought was a flippant answer, that I mumbled an obligatory goodbye and hung up the phone. The more I pondered her curt sentence, however, the more her words illuminated my problem. Attempting to build a better life, I had really constructed a prison for myself. Finally admitting our own complicity in this pain, Kay and I sold the house and moved into a more modest one, made do with one car instead of two, I went back to teaching, and Kay stayed home with our three young children. We did not have a nickel extra at the end of the month, but we enjoyed some of the best years of our marriage – all because we acknowledged we had trapped ourselves and we simply needed to let some things go.

On a much larger and important scale, all humans are trapped in prisons of their own making until they admit their sin and allow Jesus Christ to unburden them. The whole march of the Bible is toward a God who wants nothing more than to restore what is broken in humanity and mend the fractures it has caused in our relationships with God and one another. Our biggest challenge is to climb down the ladder of our pride and let God do what only can be done through the crucified Christ. The glittering citadels of our false egos will have to crumble in order to be replaced by the persons of distinct purpose and resplendent beauty we were fashioned to be, a beauty reflecting the awesomely loving and generous God who created us.

Galatians 2:20 (NRSV)

20 and it is no longer I who live, but it is Christ who lives in me. And the life I now live in the flesh I live by faith in the Son of God, who loved me and gave himself for me.

Discussion Questions for Chapter 2
Why is Jesus Christ the Focus of Our Faith?

Our Stories
Remember a time you felt trapped. What did you do about it?

Reading Review
1. Do you ever feel purposelessness about human life? If so, what's the root of your malaise?

2. How do we humans reject our divinely bequeathed purpose?

3. Is there a way out of this deadly trap we have set for ourselves? Why do we call the avenue out of our trap the *gospel* or the *good news*?

Bible Connections
1. Read **Genesis 1:26-27**. Right out of the gate, how does the Bible define humanity's purpose? In your own words, what do you think the author of Genesis means?

2. Read **Romans 5:6-8**. On whose faithfulness do we depend? Does Christ's "timing" surprise you? Why do we so often get the message of this passage backwards, and what is the result of doing so?

3. Read **Galatians 2:20**. According to Paul, what else happens to us when we accept this *good news* from Jesus Christ?

4. Read **1 Corinthians 2:2**. Why would Paul make such a strange statement?

Chapter 3

How Does the Holy Spirit Animate our Life in Christ?

Can I become the person I want to be?

"You've become a fanatic!" Those were pretty fierce words coming from the girl I would ask to marry me just five months later. "What has happened to you," the fury of her query almost singeing my ear through the telephone receiver?

Kay, my then girlfriend and now my wife of these past 34 years, had a right to be concerned. The young man speaking to her on the phone that spring of 1975 was not the same edition who had left for college in the summer of 1973. Something had happened to him – to me. I can vividly remember the Sunday night, alone in my dorm room, explaining frankly to the young woman I loved that I would rather be a "fanatic" than be what I was before.

What, indeed, had happened to me? The summer I departed Birmingham, AL to attend early football camp in Texas, I was afire with all the expectations and excitement of most any college freshman. I planned to experience it all, drink in every last drop of my well-earned freedom. Those hot weeks of summer preceding my departure, I had worked in a dark, steamy factory in the gloomy industrial center of my hometown. My previous four years of high school were spent in a rigorous, highly structured, military-like, mostly male boarding school on an isolated mountaintop. I was poised to break out of my childhood restraints.

Break out I did. The weekends at college started for me on Thursday and ended on Tuesday. When I was not in class or on the football field, I was drinking, dating, and partying with unrequited fervor. I played to the crowd, and my actions became all the more raucous. In the athletic dorm where I resided, my hall mates began to call me "Cowboy" because any semblance of my southern reticence had been erased in the new Wild West version of myself. One night I was on a first date with a beautiful, genteel Hispanic girl, whom I had met in my economics class. I had long wanted a date with her. At the fraternity party we attended that night, I was challenged to a Tequila drinking contest. Never one to back down in front of a crowd, I took up the challenge, which consisted of drinking a shot of Tequila then performing some athletic feat, such as completing twenty-five pushups or remaining in a head-stand for three minutes. To the increasing horror of my date, I won the contest on the twenty-first shot of Tequila. I could have easily died that night due to alcohol poisoning; instead I simply vomited all over my date's mother's carefully manicured rose bushes. After that, the girl refused to even acknowledge my presence in the classroom or hallways; even so, I did not yet see the dark clouds gathering around my life. What I would come to understand was that my life was like that beautiful rose bush now covered with the filth I had put there.

My hedonistic lifestyle persisted into my sophomore year. Then, in a pre-season scrimmage against Southwest Texas State University, I caught a pass over the middle, only to be pummeled by their safety and middle linebacker. I saw stars, and six medical examinations later would discover that ferocious hit would end my football career.

For a while I intensified my debauchery in a protest against my dethronement as a collegiate athlete. Then seemingly out of nowhere that fall, a round, soft-spoken, black bearded man, whose name I cannot even recall, invited me to meet with him in the student center that next Sunday night. I knew him to be a volunteer with one of the campus Christian ministries, so I politely responded that I might come – not intending in the least to make the appointment. However, Sunday night arrived, and I was uncharacteristically alone in my room. At 7:55,

I meandered up to the student center where I found him expectantly sitting there at a table for two.

Once we got beyond the pleasantries of our initial meeting, my long anesthetized anger began to surface. I peppered him with predictable questions and confident proclamations: "Why are there different religions anyway?" "Jesus, Buddha, Mohammed are the same guy in different clothes." "What will happen to all those people who have never even heard the name of Jesus?" The chubby bearded man allowed me to rage on, deftly and sensitively answering my questions when I would dare take a breath and let him.

Finally, I said, "Why do you need religion as long as you are a good person?" I then swallowed hard and quit my rantings because I knew, regardless of his answer; I was not a good person. The blow to my insides was harder than the one I had recently received on that Texas football field. I was falling. Thankfully, that funny round man was there to catch me.

For months of Sunday nights, he listened to me, tutored me, prayed with me, allowed me to cry, and engaged my questions with the tender authenticity I desperately needed. Our only textbook was the Bible, and he showed me that our most urgent questions are engaged there. Of course, my deepest question was how could I become the person I really wanted to be instead of this imposter who was destructively gallivanting around in my clothes. The answer from scripture was abundantly clear but seemingly far too simple: I could not become good on my own, but that power of God found in Jesus Christ who extended Himself to be tortured and murdered on the Cross, power such that death could not contain him in a rock-hewn tomb, that same awesome power was available to me. God could transform me – a narcissistic, selfish, caustic 20 year-old college brat – from the inside out. I only had to get my pride out of the way so the Holy Spirit could do God's incredible work within me.

The succeeding weeks with the little round man became my honeymoon with God. The New Testament I quickly discovered was not merely a book full of historical nuggets fit for museum gazing, but one with stories that can come to life in a person now. The Holy Spirit commenced to reorient my life from top to bottom. While I was not and am not a candidate for sainthood, I ceased loathing myself and began to like the man staring back at me in the mirror.

The honeymoon, however, came to a screeching halt on that Sunday night in the mid-spring of 1975. Just when I was fully enjoying the cocoon of grace my teacher had wrapped around me, he looked across that familiar table there in the student center and said, "Pat, it's time you started teaching your own Bible study." Almost choking on my fries, I frantically retorted, "What would I teach? Who would come?" He confidently answered, "Teach what you know and teach who you know."

I walked out of the student center in a stupor. Who would want to attend a Bible study taught by the least likely Christian teacher on campus? Over the next few days, I would learn that a lot of people would, if for nothing else than the novelty of a hedonist turned Bible teacher. I invited athletes, friends, girls I had dated. Almost everyone agreed to meet for the appointed hour on Tuesday afternoons. That first Sunday night, however, I doubted anyone would heed my invitation. So I called Kay at her dorm room in Alabama to tell her my plans and receive some encouragement. That's when she said, "You've become a fanatic!"

I may have exuded some self-assured fanatical zeal to Kay on the phone that night, but I had no confidence whatsoever in my ability to teach the Bible to anyone. I decided, therefore, to keep to the main road and tell my fledging class about the most colorful and fanatical personality in the scripture – Saul of Tarsus, later to be renamed Paul. If my collegiate colleagues were befuddled and somewhat skeptical about my turn-about, Paul's story would surely shock them much more. After all, Paul feverishly arrested first century Christians in order to imprison and murder them. During one such believers' round up, Paul was knocked onto the dirt of the Damascus Road and blinded by an encounter with the resurrected Christ. Paul's conversion of life was powerful and immediate. In fact, his life change was so radical that other Christians at that time had a very hard time believing it. The history book of the New Testament, the Acts of the Apostles, records the first skeptical responses to Paul's unlikely conversion:

Acts 9:17-30 (NRSV)

17 So Ananias went and entered the house. He laid his hands on Saul and said, "Brother Saul, the Lord Jesus, who appeared to you on your way here, has sent me so that you may regain your sight and be filled with the Holy Spirit." 18 And immediately something like scales fell from his eyes, and his sight was restored. Then he got up and was baptized, 19 and after taking some food, he regained his strength. For several days he was with the disciples in Damascus, 20 and immediately he began to proclaim Jesus in the synagogues, saying, "He is the Son of God." 21 All who heard him were amazed and said, "Is not this the man who made havoc in Jerusalem among those who invoked this name? And has he not come here for the purpose of bringing them bound before the chief priests?" 22 Saul became increasingly more powerful and confounded the Jews who lived in Damascus by proving that Jesus was the Messiah. 23 After some time had passed, the Jews plotted to kill him, 24 but their plot became known to Saul. They were watching the gates day and night so that they might kill him; 25 but his disciples took him by night and let him down through an opening in the wall, lowering him in a basket. 26 When he had come to Jerusalem, he attempted to join the disciples; and they were all afraid of him, for they did not believe that he was a disciple. 27 But Barnabas took him, brought him to the apostles, and described for them how on the road he had seen the Lord, who had spoken to him, and how in Damascus he had spoken boldly in the name of Jesus. 28 So he went in and out among them in Jerusalem, speaking boldly in the name of the Lord. 29 He spoke and argued with the Hellenists; but they were attempting to kill him. 30 When the believers learned of it, they brought him down to Caesarea and sent him off to Tarsus.

Paul's life change is so complete and so powerful that within a very short time there are two conspiracies to murder him. His 180° reversal of life is more than his old cronies can take. The greatest enemy of Christ had become his champion. Paul's life moved from one being bent on destruction of others to one centered upon saving them. No one is more surprised by this transformation than Paul himself.

1 Corinthians 15:8-11 (NRSV)

8 Last of all, as to one untimely born, he (Christ) appeared also to me. 9 For I am the least of the apostles, unfit to be called an apostle, because I persecuted the church of God. 10 But by the grace of God I am what I am, and his grace toward me has not been in vain. On the contrary, I worked harder than any of them—though it was not I, but the grace of God that is with me. 11 Whether then it was I or they, so we proclaim and so you have come to believe.

Can I become more like Christ?

It is far too easy to relegate familiar stories like Paul's to the past, as if God was in overdrive then but is content to let us muddle along now. Furthermore, the story about my own college days resonates with the stories of many others who supposedly were "sowing the wild oats of youth." If we are not careful, we will imagine God has either become tame in this modern age or now has lowered expectations for us. As Paul himself matured in his faith, he noted that we are to "dress up in Christ." (Galatians 3:27) The Holy Spirit continuously works with us so that we can be transformed more and more into the image of Christ. Ultimately, God's desire is not just to make us good but also to refashion us into the image of the Son. Perhaps the most astonishing story of transformation that I have ever read took place in a nursing home only a few years ago.

It all began when the young man asked at the nurses' station for directions to a Mr. McAllister's room. The nurses, the clerk, even the aides stopped in their tracks. The usually busy, noisy work area became as quiet as a cathedral. No one asked directions to Mr. McAllister's room, no one called him, and no one had ever hinted that they wanted to see him. No one, they thought, should want to see him – ever.

In 1974, Mr. McAllister had abducted a boy, shot him, stabbed him, burned him with cigarette butts, and then left him to die. The boy had survived the ordeal but had lost sight in one eye due to the gunshot wound. After some time, Mr. McAllister had confessed his guilt to the authorities.

The staff at the North Miami nursing home was, therefore, rightfully stunned that anyone would come to visit the pitiful old man. What would eventually surprise them far more was the young man standing at the nurses' station that day was the young boy who had been tortured by the old man in 1974. The young man, Mr. Carrier, now married with children, had learned the whereabouts of Mr. McAllister through the efforts of Major Scherer, the investigating detective some fifteen years ago.

The New York Times later chronicled the unlikely meeting between the two men. In that first encounter, the account reads, "Mr. McAllister began to cry when he realized the young man before him was the boy he had hurt and abandoned. When asked what he had done, he sort of gasped and said, 'I left him there,' and began to cry. Mr. McAllister then said he was sorry, and Mr. Carrier told him that he forgave him and that from now on there would be nothing like anger or revenge between them, nothing except a new friendship."

The Times piece concludes with Mr. Carrier stating, "'I'm glad he (Mr. McAllister) was able to put the past behind him. I tried to let him know that he had a friend.' And he did. Mr. Carrier visited him regularly, prayed with him, read with him, and then three weeks later when he died, took care of the funeral arrangements."[8]

Fantastic stories proceeding from Mt. Olympus have got nothing on this tale. Mr. Carrier's response to the heinous, brutal, unthinkable acts done to him was to forgive his torturer and repair the breach between them. Looking at the story from a human point of view, I

---

[8] Alanson B. Houghton, "Model of Forgiveness" (The Living Church, March 2, 1997), p.2. Quoting New York Times article "Forgiven and Befriended by His Victim, Attacker Dies".

contend it should be the other way around – Mr. McAllister should be the one attempting to restore the almost impassable breach between them. However, looking at it from the God-ward side, I begin to see the divine pattern of the young man's actions. The landscape appears different from the cross.

Luke 23: 33-34 (RSV)

And when they came to the place which is called The Skull,
there they crucified him, and the criminals, one on the right
and one on the left. And Jesus said, 'Father, forgive them;
for they know not what they are doing.'

God's divine pattern, as expressed through Jesus Christ, becomes the divine reversal. The laws of "an eye for an eye, a tooth for a tooth," of people receiving reasonable justice, is overturned by the one who receives the very worst we humans can dole out. Instead of giving us what we deserve, our just desserts, we receive mercy and restoration. From the cross, Jesus looks upon us, his pitiful offenders, and extends to us what we so badly need but cannot give ourselves. Something much, much bigger than humanity is at work here.

About the time we finally get honest about our condition and come to grips with the unfathomable gift of mercy that has been extended to us, we begin to wonder how we can personally receive the power of grace and forgiveness working in Jesus Christ. How can we manifest the unconditional love so obviously present in Mr. Carrier? On an intellectual level, we know that returning hurt for hurt, jab for jab, insult for insult just perpetuates the mad cycle of unfinished retribution. As Christians, we know, too, that although our deeds warrant judgment – our God is holy, thus we are to be holy – nevertheless, we have received unmerited grace. We are no longer under condemnation because God's love has been extended through the cross. Sadly, while we know these things, we continue in our selfish and destructive ways. Our only hope for transformation is that the same divine power operative in Christ may become active in us. The hope is not a pipe dream, for the gift of the Holy Spirit will cause the unconditional love of Christ to be expressed through us. We do not have to continue our cycle of sinful, painful actions. The power of God desires to live within us.

The power and promise of the Holy Spirit is vividly expressed at the end of John's gospel. The resurrected Jesus visits the disciples as they are huddled behind closed doors. They are frozen by fear and despair due to the horror of the crucifixion just three days before.

John 20: 19-23 (RSV)

On the evening of that day, the first day of the week, the doors being shut where the disciples were, for fear of the Jews, Jesus stood among them and said to them, 'Peace be with you.' When he had said this, he showed them his hands and his side. Then the disciples were glad when they saw the Lord. Jesus said to them again, 'Peace be with you. As the Father has sent me, even so I send you.' And when he had said this be breathed on them, and said to them, 'Receive the Holy Spirit. If you forgive the sins of any, they are forgiven; if you retain the sins of any, they are retained.'

The imagery in this passage is sated with personal symbolism. The disciples are locked behind the closed doors of fear, anguish, anger, regret, and defeat. Then he breathes his very own life into them and sends them off to forgive as he has so abundantly forgiven. Jesus shows the disciples his wounds, not so much as proof of his identity, as much as proof of what extreme lengths God will go to express His love. Just as God breathes into the nostrils of the first human being to give him physical life (Genesis 2:7), Jesus Christ breathes onto the disciples to give them new life, a life that no longer keeps score of rights and wrongs, but rather puts its energy into lavishly loving. This is the new life available to us through the gift of the Holy Spirit.

How can I climb out of this rut I'm in?

While the extraordinary gift of the Holy Spirit "to forgive those who have trespassed against us" is somewhat plausible, we have a harder time believing the deadly habits we have formed can be transformed. We may begin the day with the best of intentions, yet with the first irritating gesture from a family member, friend, teacher, or co-worker, we react with the same destructive habits. We wonder after these routine encounters, who watching me would ever desire to be a Christian? What difference has my faith in Christ made in my daily life? Our questions resonate with the honest admission of St. Paul, written many years after his blinding encounter with Christ on the Damascus Road.

Romans 7:13-20 (The Message)

What I can't understand about myself is that I decide one way, but then I act another, doing things I absolutely despise. So if I can't be trusted to figure out what is best for myself and then do it, it becomes obvious that God's command is necessary. But I need something more! For if I know the law but still can't keep it, and if the power of sin keeps on sabotaging my best intentions, I obviously need help! I realize that I do not have what it takes. I can will it, but I cannot do it. I decide to do good, but I don't really do it; I decide not to do bad, but then I do it anyway. My decisions, such as they are, don't result in actions. Something has gone wrong deep within me and gets the better of me every time.

Paul's honesty is unnerving, but he is right: the more we try to do the right thing the worse it gets. Trusting in our own power, we simply become more consumed with self, not less. In effect, the more we trust in our own power to perfect ourselves, the more we have made the person in the mirror God. We are on most dangerous ground. We were fashioned to be Holy as God is Holy, but only through the gift of God's own self in the Holy Spirit. Paul, therefore, answers the conundrum he espouses in Romans 7 with a liberating response.

Romans 8:5-11 (The Message)

Those who think they can do it on their own end up obsessed with measuring their own moral muscle but never get around to exercising it in real life. Those who trust God's action in them find that God's Spirit is in them – living and breathing God! Obsession with self in these matters is a dead end; attention to God leads us out into the open, into a spacious, free life. Focusing on the self is the opposite of focusing on God. Anyone absorbed in self ignores God, ends up thinking more about self than God...It stands to reason, doesn't it, that if the alive-and-present God who raised Jesus from the dead moves into your life, he'll do the same thing in you that he did in Jesus, bringing you alive to himself. When God lives and breathes in you (and he does, as surely as he did in Jesus), you are delivered from that dead life. With his Spirit living in you, your body will be alive as Christ's.

The gift we have so badly wanted and needed we have had all the while. Those of us who believe that God delivered Jesus Christ from death and trust in that abounding love, have already received the Holy Spirit. We just have to open up the locked doors of our hearts and close the door of our voracious narcissism. God desires to dress us up in Himself.

Discussion Questions for Chapter 3
How Does the Holy Spirit Animate Our Life in Christ?

Our Stories

What's keeping you from being the person you want to be? Be honest and specific.

Reading Review

1. What can at first be painful about our new life in Christ?

2. How can we undergo a second birth of sorts?

3. Who may well be the worst enemy we will encounter in our new Spirit-led life in Christ?

Bible Connections

1. Read **Romans 7:15-20**. Why is this admission from Paul brutally true for both him and us?

2. Read **Genesis 2:7** and then read **John 20:19-23**. According to the authors of Genesis and John, what winds must we catch to become fully alive?

3. Read **Luke 23:32-34** and then read **Acts 7:54-60**. At the end, what specific transformation took place in Stephen? Can we expect as much?

4. Read **1 Corinthians 12:4-11**. For what main purpose are we given *spiritual gifts*? Can you name one of yours?

Chapter 4

Why Do We Have the Church?

What is the Church?

It was December 23 and outside it was seventeen degrees, bitterly cold by Texas standards. I was huddled in my office trying to compose a riveting sermon for Christmas Eve, but had failed during the last hour to get beyond "In the name of the Father, the Son, and the Holy Spirit." Before things got really dire and I started throwing things, Chad walked in. Chad was a member of the parish and a dear friend, who had joined his family in a local real estate business.

By the look on his face, I could tell this was not a social call. "Pat, can you take a drive with me? There is something you need to see," he said as more demand than request. I put down my pencil and followed him to his Ford Bronco. Chad drove west about fifteen miles beyond the city limits.

Chad explained as he neared the destination, "I found this while I was inspecting some property earlier this afternoon. He then parked in front of what I supposed was a long abandoned shack. The home, with only tiny flecks of white paint remaining on it, had collapsed on all but one corner. The two of us squeezed our way into the interior where I discovered my friend's purpose. Sitting on a damp, mildewed couch in the only un-collapsed room was an African-American mother and her two young sons huddled around a blue *Maxwell House* coffee can that had four of five charcoals burning in it. A ragged quilt was spread across their three sets of shoulders.

Aghast by the sight and the knowledge that the three of them would freeze that night if not moved, I stuttered, "Would you like us to take you some place warm?" The mother said nothing, but nodded in reply. In moments she put all of their belongings into one brown paper grocery bag, and the three of them followed Chad and me to the car.

A few phone calls later, we had arranged through a local assistance agency for the trio to have warm, comfortable lodging for the remainder of the winter. The next night at the Christmas Eve worship services the men of the parish pledged to provide the family a new home by spring's end.

Good to their word, the men bought a mobile home in need of rehabilitation. They then moved the home onto the family's property, purposely placing it right in front of their dilapidated shanty so that it could no longer be seen from the road. Then on the appointed Saturday, some thirty men of the church met at the mobile home intent on restoring it and moving in the family by the end of the day. I remember it as an almost perfect morning. The *Skill* saws seemed to be singing and the hammers kept time as we worked ankle deep in the spring mud. I was a young, idealistic, newly ordained man, and I kept saying to myself, "This is what the church is all about!" The words were like a mantra resounding repeatedly and joyfully in my head.

Accentuating my joy was the younger of the two brothers, who had become my shadow that day. He had experienced a very hard winter due to his aggravated asthma. He had spent most of those days either in the bed or in the hospital. He was excited to be running around outdoors. He was ecstatic about his new home. Every time we would circle the southwest corner of the mobile home, he would point at a small aluminum casement window and query breathlessly, "Pat, is that my room? Is that my room?" I would nod and think if we had not rescued that boy from his unheated, mold-ridden, falling-down shack, he would have died that winter. Also, I do not think I ever saw anyone so expectant on account of a faded brown and white, very used mobile home.

Although I hid it somewhat, I, like that little boy, was so exhilarated that my feet felt as if they were walking atop the mud. Sometime around 2:00 PM, however, I noticed the sound of the work had ceased. I looked up from my task of cleaning ten year-old grit off of windows to see all of the men circled around a barrel-chested deputy sheriff. After a few moments, the leader of our men's group stepped to the front of the crowd and addressed me, "Pat, this here deputy says the mother of these two boys is a prostitute and she will just turn this place into her new whore house."

I felt as if someone had knocked the wind out of me. In one sentence, I had gone from a perfect experience of church to a horrible one. My youthful idealism and zeal was no match for the confrontation. OK, I thought, so perhaps the mother prostituted herself. Considering their former desperation, it was not hard to imagine. Anyway, was that any reason to allow her beautiful children to die? I didn't have the presence of mind to say any of that, but I did muster a question. While pointing at the southwest corner of the mobile home, I asked, "Which one of you is going to tell this little boy that's not his room over there?"

Following the question, there was grumbling, some of the men left, but most remained. Yet the laughter and the music of the day were gone. It was nightfall when we finished. Chad and I left in his Bronco. Physically and emotionally exhausted, I looked back at the brown and white mobile home as we drove off the property. The lights were on, and framed in the small metal window of his room was the smiling, black toothy face of the boy. He appeared more a prince looking out over the ramparts of his castle than the beleaguered son of a whore.

That experience in the spring mud of Texas is like others I've had in the church. About the time I'm swept up in the church's majesty and generosity, I am dashed to the ground by its pettiness and egotism. It can be the most perfect and imperfect institution on earth. It is a supernatural assembly with an all too human face.

Jesus said very little specifically about the Church that would help us out with our hot and cold relationship with it. There is his famous assertion to Peter at Caesarea Philippi: "And I tell you that you are Peter, and on this rock I will build my church, and the gates of Hades will not prevail against it. I will give you the keys to the kingdom of heaven, and whatever you bind on earth shall be bound in heaven and whatever you loose on earth shall be loosed in heaven." (Matthew 16:18-19) Nevertheless, Jesus adds no additional descriptions or instructions about the proposed structure of the church he will leave on earth. Then again, perhaps Peter himself is to be the blueprint, the universal human face of the emerging church. He who is called the rock is more like *play-dough* when adversity hits Jesus and his twelve disciples. The times Jesus really needs Peter, the rock is either snoozing or denying he ever knew Jesus to any who asks him. (Matthew 26:30-46; 69-75) Peter deserts Jesus just as the Temple bureaucrats are busy slapping him physically and verbally, and that is merely a light prelude to torture at the hands of the highly practiced Romans.

As Jesus approaches his death at the trash heap known as Golgotha, spineless Peter is absent. Some "rock"? How ironic that Jesus, after his resurrection, seeks out Peter, who, even in that short amount of time, has surrendered his calling as a disciple in order to return to his safer, more predictable life as a fisherman. Jesus cooks breakfast for Peter and six others right there on the shore of the Sea of Galilee where they had spent so much of those three years during their unusual rabbi's ministry. After they have eaten, Jesus takes Peter aside to question him.

John 21:15-19 (NRSV)

15 When they had finished breakfast, Jesus said to Simon Peter, "Simon son of John, do you love me more than these?" He said to him, "Yes, Lord; you know that I love you." Jesus said to him, "Feed my lambs." 16 A second time he said to him, "Simon son of John, do you love me?" He said to him, "Yes, Lord; you know that I love you." Jesus said to him, "Tend my sheep." 17 He said to him the third time, "Simon son of John, do you love me?" Peter felt hurt because he said to him the third time, "Do you love me?" And he said to him, "Lord, you know everything; you know that I love you." Jesus said to him, "Feed my sheep. 18 Very truly, I tell you, when you were younger, you used to fasten your own belt and to go wherever you wished. But when you grow old, you will stretch out your hands, and someone else will fasten a belt around you and take you where you do not wish to go."19 (He said this to indicate the kind of death by which he would glorify God.) After this he said to him, "Follow me."

Note that Jesus asks Peter three times if Peter loves him. All three times Peter answers "yes" in what becomes an act of confession and forgiveness. His three denials of Jesus and other faithless acts have been met with grace and a renewed call. Peter is given the "keys to the kingdom of heaven" because all of us knocking on the door of faith are just like him - woefully short of the mark. The church is filled to overflowing with Peters, and all of us get what we don't deserve - the grace of forgiveness and reconciliation with God plus a call to a meaningful life. Christ seeks us the way a groom seeks a bride he cherishes. The church is not perfect then, just loved. The church is loved into goodness, and we are at our best when we extend grace such that we received. Holy Scripture illustrates the power of this reciprocal love using an example from our most intimate human relationship:

Ephesians 5:25-31 (NRSV)

25 Husbands, love your wives, just as Christ loved the church and gave himself up for her, 26 in order to make her holy by cleansing her with the washing of water by the word, 27 so as to present the church to himself in splendor, without a spot or wrinkle or anything of the kind—yes, so that she may be holy and without blemish.28 In the same way, husbands should love their wives as they do their own bodies. He who loves his wife loves himself.29 For no one ever hates his own body, but he nourishes and tenderly cares for it, just as Christ does for the church, 30 because we are members of his body.31 "For this reason a man will leave his father and mother and be joined to his wife, and the two will become one flesh."

Unlike Jesus, Paul says loads about the church, and he uses a great deal of body language when referring to it. He sees the assembly of Christian believers on earth as far more than just a group of people with a common purpose and leader. Paul asserts that Christians are collectively grafted into the person of Christ. The Good News, the liberating news of the gospel, is what attracts people into the Church. However, the gathering is far different than some civic organization that just happens to have a steeple and cross atop its meetinghouse instead of moose horns or the like. The Church is of divine origin and substance. Christ is the head and we, his sometimes-fickle followers, are his body. Nevertheless, there is far more to the church than meets the eye. On the more catholic side of the church, there has been much ado about the "real presence" of Christ, particularly as it relates to the sacrament of Holy Eucharist. Additionally, on the more Protestant side of the church, much has been stated about how the Church obscures the true message of the gospel of Christ and the radically good news that proceeds from him. The scripture testifies that the Church is indelibly yoked to both – the actual presence of Christ and the good news that proceeds from him. Christians come together, not because they need their weekly "fill-up" of the sacraments or because they require expert Bible instruction or even because they happen to like the people in a particular parish. No, Christians come together because that is where Christ can be found – "in the midst of them," as Christ said himself. (Matthew 18:20) Carl Braaten of the Center for Catholic and Evangelical Theology writes, "The church is not merely an external instrument, but it is ontologically (its very being) the body of Christ. The church is therefore a reality within the fullness of the Gospel. The church through Word and Sacraments conveys the real presence of Christ, the whole Christ, head and body, Christ and his church. Those who have fellowship with Christ will also have fellowship with each other. Believing in Christ and belonging to the church go together."[9]

---

[9] Carl E. Braaten, "The Gospel Proviso" in <u>Ancient and Postmodern Christianity</u>, ed. Kenneth Tanner and Christopher A. Hall (Downers Grove, IL: Intervarsity Press, 2002) 212.

Consider the men of my former parish and the mobile home incident. Any number of organizations could have purchased, moved, and restored that used, brown and white mobile home more efficiently than the church. Yet the men came to that little plot of ground in Texas and the presence of Christ was amongst them. To encounter those men that steamy day upon the spring mud is to have fellowship with Christ. On the other hand, the men exercised an all too predictable response to a family in dire need, and almost, in fact, turned their backs on them. Their actions are hauntingly reminiscent of Peter, and yet God chooses to act through the frailty and utter fallibility of human beings.

How does the church work?

Human weakness is not the bad news about the "good news." Quite the opposite! The reason God is born into the world as one of us becomes much clearer when viewing it from ground level. Jesus Christ becomes walking around proof that God desires to work through humanity. It is messy because there are battalions upon battalions of all of us *Peter's* with whom God has to work. Peter's change is witness to the world that others can be changed and put to work bearing Christ to those many hopelessly huddled in the dark, cold corners.

Ephesians 2:8-18 (NRSV)

8 For by grace you have been saved through faith, and this is not your own doing; it is the gift of God—9 not the result of works, so that no one may boast. 10 For we are what he has made us, created in Christ Jesus for good works, which God prepared beforehand to be our way of life.

Certainly, on the top ten list of God's radical ideas is that it takes God's own creatures to complete God's purpose. God's work on earth will not be completed without us. Jesus, then, takes on human flesh not only to save us, but also to model what the church is to be. The work of God is entrusted to humanity. The Quakers are on target when they say, "Christ has no hands but ours."

The radical notion that the church completes God's purpose is continued in God's intention for each one of us. We complete one another. The western notion of rugged individualism is contrary to scripture. The faith community exercises the power of God because alone we are inadequate. God's purpose will not be realized in divine solitude nor will ours be on earth. We need each other and not just because one person is good with a hammer and another with a saw. Our spiritual composition is such that we come to full life in communion with others. It is our life together that witnesses most powerfully to a fractured world. John Bunyan, the great seventeenth century preacher and author, was greeting his congregation at the front doors after worship one Sunday when a woman said, "Rev. Bunyan, your sermon was marvelous." "Yes," he responded, "the devil has already told me that." The glorification of the individual, even in the accomplishment of godly work, is not the witness of the church. The primary witness proceeds from the body. We come to life in the faith community because we are completed in it. Thus, the church's message to the world is that we can be healed by being made whole within the community.

Romans 12:3-8 (NRSV)

3 For by the grace given to me I say to everyone among you not to think of yourself more highly than you ought to think, but to think with sober judgment, each according to the measure of faith that God has assigned. 4 For as in one body we have many members, and not all the members have the same function, 5 so we, who are many, are one body in Christ, and individually we are members one of another. 6 We have gifts that differ according to the grace given to us: prophecy, in proportion to faith; 7 ministry, in ministering; the teacher, in teaching; 8 the exhorter, in exhortation; the giver, in generosity; the leader, in diligence; the compassionate, in cheerfulness.

God working through the body of believers is as apparent in the Old Testament and in the new. The patriarch Jacob is renamed *Israel* to signify the collective nature of God's call and care. (Genesis 32:22-28) The Old Testament is rife with stories about heroes, judges, military leaders, and prophets; however, they are given power by God to shepherd the body of people. The most dramatic of these calls is issued to Moses as he was enjoying the anonymous life in Midian. "The cry of the Israelites has come to me," says God from the burning bush; "I have also seen how the Egyptians oppress them. So come, I will send you to Pharaoh to bring my people, the Israelites, out of Egypt." (Exodus 3:9-10) Nevertheless, as we read on in the Old Testament, we discover it is Peter's story in spades. Israel cannot seem to ever be faithful to God, even though God delivered them from the strongest nation on earth, and gave them a land of their own that has been nicely cultivated by others. Furthermore, Israel was granted a special relationship with God through the gift of the Law. The Law was never meant to be a legal litmus test of who was in and who was out. Rather, it was meant to be a special window in the nature of God through which Israel could realize corporate fellowship and participate in God. Additionally, the body of Israel was fashioned to be inclusive from the beginning. Israel picked up an array of different people as they traveled toward the Promised Land, and they were all engrafted into Israel. Joshua, the valiant guerilla warfare general of Israel, bespeaks this breadth of the community in a celebration speech after a great military victory. It is important to note that the Law is the centerpiece of the celebration, reminding the diverse assembly of people who and Whose they really are.

Joshua 8:32-35 (NRSV)

32 And there, in the presence of the Israelites, Joshua wrote on the stones a copy of the law of Moses, which he had written.33 All Israel, alien as well as citizen, with their elders and officers and their judges, stood on opposite sides of the ark in front of the Levitical priests who carried the ark of the covenant of the LORD, half of them in front of Mount

*Gerizim and half of them in front of Mount Ebal, as Moses
the servant of the LORD had commanded at the first, that
they should bless the people of Israel.34 And afterward he
read all the words of the law, blessings and curses, according
to all that is written in the book of the law.35 There was
not a word of all that Moses commanded that Joshua did
not read before all the assembly of Israel, and the women,
and the little ones, and the aliens who resided among them.*

The Hebrew prophets provide a bridge between the Old Testament notion of believers centered on the Law in fidelity with God and our understanding of Paul's body of believers centered on Jesus Christ as savior. Fully half of the Old Testament is the narratives of the prophets urging, threatening, cajoling, even begging Israel to renew their faithfulness to God through that special window of the Law they alone have been given. It is painful to read the prophets' words because they remind us that human beings have a hard time getting it right. The Old Testament is an incredibly honest book! My personal favorite prophet is Hosea. He is given an outrageous symbolic act to carry out for God: marry a prostitute. Hosea does so, and the outcome is predicable. She remains unfaithful, courts other lovers, has children by those lovers, and finally runs away from Hosea and the family. God orders an even more contemptible act when Hosea is compelled to go find his wife and renew his marriage with her. Of course, the symbolism in the prophet's tale is obvious. Israel is the prostitute. The community saved by God and led into a special relationship with God plays the whore. (Hosea 6:4) God's intention, however, is acted through Hosea. Though Israel deserts God for other lovers – material prosperity, sexual license, and power avenues – God seeks them again and again.

Hosea 11:1-4, 8-9 (NRSV)

*1 When Israel was a child, I loved him,
and out of Egypt I called my son.
2 The more I called them,*

the more they went from me;
they kept sacrificing to the Baals,
and offering incense to idols.
3 Yet it was I who taught Ephraim to walk,
I took them up in my arms;
but they did not know that I healed them.
4 I led them with cords of human kindness,
with bands of love.
I was to them like those
who lift infants to their cheeks.
I bent down to them and fed them.
8 How can I give you up, Ephraim?
How can I hand you over, O Israel?
How can I make you like Admah?
How can I treat you like Zeboiim?
My heart recoils within me;
my compassion grows warm and tender.
9 I will not execute my fierce anger;
I will not again destroy Ephraim;
for I am God and no mortal,
the Holy One in your midst,
and I will not come in wrath.

Hosea illustrates the essential continuity between the Old and New Testaments' understanding of the faith community. People did not and have not changed. We abandon God for those selfsame lovers again and again. Neither does God change. God's intention to seek us, save us, and restore us to an intimate relationship with God remains constant. The work of the church, therefore, is portrayed in the prophetic acts of Hosea. The body of Christ is to constantly seek those who are lost and restore to them the fellowship God has always intended for them. As we seek others, we must continually remember that we are being sought, too. No arrogance is plausible in the body. Grace has sought us. Grace has healed us. The church's work is to be Christ's vessel of grace.

Colossians 3:12-17

12 As God's chosen ones, holy and beloved, clothe
yourselves with compassion, kindness, humility, meekness,
and patience. 13 Bear with one another and, if anyone
has a complaint against another, forgive each other; just
as the Lord has forgiven you, so you also must forgive. 14
Above all, clothe yourselves with love, which binds
everything together in perfect harmony. 15 And let the
peace of Christ rule in your hearts, to which indeed you
were called in the one body. And be thankful. 16 Let the
word of Christ dwell in you richly; teach and admonish
one another in all wisdom; and with gratitude in your
hearts sing psalms, hymns, and spiritual songs to God. 17
And whatever you do, in word or deed, do everything in
the name of the Lord Jesus, giving thanks to God the
Father through him.

What is the Point of Christian Worship?

The church then is the community of those who acknowledge that they have been sought and healed by God. The community is born out of honesty and humility yet sustained by thanksgiving and praise. The church's corporate acts of mercy proceed from its collective celebrations. Very simply, the church is in the praise business. All of the faith community's good works are fostered by our thanksgiving to God. Through the work of Jesus Christ, God does for us what we cannot do for ourselves. In grateful response we simply continue the work – doing for others what they are unable to do for themselves. Therefore, the broken people we serve are not objectified by us. No, indeed, they are simply added to the church's celebration. Even the church's most menial work is an expression of praise.

The first song recorded in the Bible is the straightforward praise song of Miriam, the sister of Moses and Aaron. Her exclamatory verse is offered spontaneously when she and the rest of the Hebrew slaves reach the far shore of the Red Sea. Finally out of reach of Pharaoh and his fearful horde of cavalry, Miriam spontaneously leads the celebration of those freed by God.

Exodus 15:19-21 (NRSV)

19 When the horses of Pharaoh with his chariots and his chariot drivers went into the sea, the LORD brought back the waters of the sea upon them; but the Israelites walked through the sea on dry ground.20 Then the prophet Miriam, Aaron's sister, took a tambourine in her hand; and all the women went out after her with tambourines and with dancing.21 And Miriam sang to them:
"Sing to the LORD, for he has triumphed gloriously;
horse and rider he has thrown into the sea."

God not only has freed the Hebrews from the most powerful nation on earth, but God has given the people an identity as well. Very likely the word *Hebrew* is derived from *'Apiru*, which means an assorted collection of displaced people, a polite way of stating that the people God rescued from Pharaoh are a rag-tag bunch of refugees.[10] However, once God delivers them, they are made *Israel*, a community in a special relationship with God. Like their ancestor Jacob, they have come through their own struggle and been given an identity and purpose.

The powers of slavery that would suck the life out of Israel cannot be defeated without God. Those same powers of un-life in different clothing threaten to suck life away for modern humanity as well. God is faithful to deliver us, and our response should be praise and genuine celebration. So God is not vain or keeping a ledger of our gratuities or exercising a need for insatiable human tribute. Coming together to praise God will keep us from worshiping lesser gods that cannot save us. Just a few hundred words after Miriam offers her song to the newly created faith community, God extends to them the gift of the Law. The

---

[10] Benhard W. Anderson, <u>Understanding the Old Testament: Fourth Edition</u> (Englewood Cliffs, NJ: Prentice-Hall, 1957) 39.

very first commandment, as recorded in Exodus 20: "And God spoke these words saying, 'I am the Lord your God, who brought you out of the land of Egypt, out of the house of bondage. You shall have no other Gods before me.'" The church's work to praise God keeps us from so eagerly chasing the false, impotent gods of power, sensation, material wealth, and others.

Psalm 146:1-4 (NRSV)

1 Praise the LORD!
Praise the LORD, O my soul!
2 I will praise the LORD as long as I live;
I will sing praises to my God all my life long.
3 Do not put your trust in princes,
in mortals, in whom there is no help.
4 When their breath departs, they return to the earth;
on that very day their plans perish.

Humanity receives the benefit of praise. The act of praising God takes us out of ourselves. Oddly enough, our thanksgiving to God in humble admission that we are unable to save ourselves makes authentic celebration possible. Praise is the posture of the Christian. Praise is the primary element of the church's worship because it bespeaks the dynamic nature of Christian life. The church is a people in awe of what God has done for us and expectant of what God will do for us. We have no right to hold our possessions or our *selves* tightly to our chests. We praise God with outstretched arms in ecstatic acknowledgement that all things and all people that delight us were given to us by God. Our corporate praise is our declaration of freedom. The old idols cannot hold us anymore. St. Paul offers such a declaration in his Letter to the Philippians. He had come to know that the false god he had contrived was himself, a god incapable of giving Paul the freedom and identity for which he so yearned.

Philippians 3:3-8, 4:4-7 (NRSV)

3 If anyone else has reason to be confident in the flesh, I have more:5 circumcised on the eighth day, a member of the people of Israel, of the tribe of Benjamin, a Hebrew born of Hebrews; as to the law, a Pharisee;6 as to zeal, a persecutor of the church; as to righteousness under the law, blameless.7 Yet whatever gains I had, these I have come to regard as loss because of Christ.8 More than that, I regard everything as loss because of the surpassing value of knowing Christ Jesus my Lord. For his sake I have suffered the loss of all things, and I regard them as rubbish, in order that I may gain Christ.
4 Rejoice in the Lord always; again I will say, Rejoice.5 Let your gentleness be known to everyone. The Lord is near.6 Do not worry about anything, but in everything by prayer and supplication with thanksgiving let your requests be made known to God.7 And the peace of God, which surpasses all understanding, will guard your hearts and your minds in Christ Jesus.

Often when I am counseling couples for marriage, I will ask them to name one thing that will enhance their new life together week by week. I receive all sorts of good answers ranging from taking long walks together to enjoying relaxed conversations with one another to sharing their personal thoughts by regularly writing letters to one another. I commend these good ideas and others to hopeful couples. However, I always add *worship*. If the couple will worship within the church Sunday by Sunday, they will be taken out of their selves because you cannot praise God and, at the same time, remain self -absorbed. Spouses who gratefully look beyond themselves to celebrate the grace of God remain more open to the presence and needs of their partner. Worship extends the same benefit to parenting, friendship, and other human relationships. When we wrap our arms tightly around our self, we are unable to hug anyone else. Praise is the opening of the self in response to God and thereby opens us to others.

What makes the church different from other groups?

Praise extinguishes our innate penchant for self-absorption. The church, in response to the unmerited love given to us, turns its attention outward to seek others with whom we can compassionately share our lives. Often the people we reach out to consider themselves unworthy of love, perhaps like the mother and two boys Chad and I found wrapped underneath that single blanket on that frigid December evening. Yet the church must look into the darkest, coldest corners to find the unloved for whom no one else cares. The church, therefore, is a community of seekers in the very best sense of the word. We always remember that God is passionately seeking us even as we seek others.

> 1 John 4:10-12, 19-21 (The Message)
>
> *My dear, dear friends, if God loved us like this, we certainly ought to love each other. No one has seen God, ever. But if we love one another, God dwells deeply within us, and his love becomes complete in us—perfect love!*

If anyone boasts, "I love God," and goes right on hating his brother or sister, thinking nothing of it, he is a liar. If he won't love the person he can see, how can he love the God he can't see? The command we have from Christ is blunt: Loving God includes loving people. You've got to love both.

In what amounts to Jesus' inaugural address for his public ministry, he tersely describes this central aspect of the faith community that will be gathered around him. The setting for Jesus' address is his hometown of Nazareth during the first year of his public ministry. While at worship in the town's synagogue, Jesus is invited to come forward in order to read the scripture to the assembled people. Jesus chooses to read a portion of Isaiah 61 to the home folks.

Luke 4:16-19 (NRSV)

16 When he came to Nazareth, where he had been brought up, he went to the synagogue on the sabbath day, as was his custom. He stood up to read, 17 and the scroll of the prophet Isaiah was given to him. He unrolled the scroll and found the place where it was written:
18 "The Spirit of the Lord is upon me,
because he has anointed me
to bring good news to the poor.
He has sent me to proclaim release to the captives
and recovery of sight to the blind,
to let the oppressed go free,
19 to proclaim the year of the Lord's favor."

His reading selection was certainly within bounds of the expected. However, when he finished the scripture reading, he concluded by stating, "Today this scripture has been fulfilled in your hearing." He means that the Kingdom of God is within their reach now. In that little dusty overlooked town, the presence of God can be experienced through the selfless, loving actions of the community of faith. "Seek out the poor, the captives, the blind, he says. Hold nothing back." Jesus is saying that our work will become more than what appears on the surface. Justin Martyr, writing early in the second century, stated, "He (Jesus) was merely a carpenter, making ploughs and yokes, and instructing us by such symbols of righteousness to avoid an inactive life."[11] Nevertheless, his old acquaintances and friends respond to his one line editorial as predicted. "Who does this young upstart carpenter turned rabbi think he is?" They are so angry by his presumptuous comments that they try to kill him before he leaves Nazareth. More than likely, they are angrier with themselves than at Jesus, which can be the fiercest fury.

---

[11] Justin Martyr, "Dialogue with Trypho 7.7." Ancient Christian Commentary on Scripture: Mark, Thomas C. Oden and Christopher A. Hall, eds. (Downers Grove, IL: InterVarsity Press, 1998) 79.

The church bears little resemblance to other human societies. Most other gatherings – even families for the most part – are concerned with their own self-preservation. Most all of us can recall times when we experienced the church itself as insular and blind. The church to really be church must cast its vision and care to those beyond the society. Extending ourselves into the dark places where people are badly hurting can be dirty and dangerous business. My continuing experience with those same men in Texas bears out that truth.

We recovered from our fracture over the mobile home and the supposed prostitute, and we thought we were once again open to a new challenge. One of our fellowship heard of an elderly African-American blind man whose home was in grave need of exterior repair and paint. He has lived many years in a little wood frame house on the outskirts of town. We agreed to repaint his home and replace any rotten wood we found during the job. His home was a small two-bedroom; thus, we expected to make short work of it. None of us could imagine what we would find inside his home that Saturday morning. One entire bedroom was stacked from floor to ceiling with decaying garments, newspapers, and sundry household trash. Rats the size of Chihuahuas traversed all about the home, and the stench was overwhelming. As we began to move stinking accumulated debris from that room, several of our brawny workers rushed outside to vomit up their breakfast. Every room in the house was so laden with filth that we had to call in a women's group from the parish to help us. Only the knowledge that this gentle blind man had lived in the rat-infested house for twenty-five years kept us from fleeing the scene.

When we finished our work and the men and women had left, I remained behind to speak with the man one final time. During the entire day as we worked the old black man sat in the driver's seat of a 1972 baby-blue wheel-less Cadillac parked in the center of his front yard. I parted the weeds barring the passenger-side, opened the door, and climbed in beside him. I reported that we had finished the work, and he said he had one final question – "What does it look like?"

Before I thought about what I was saying, I blurted
back, "Excuse me, sir?"
"What color is it?" "What color is my house?"
I then reported both the colors of the house and trim.
He smiled a broad satisfying grin and said, "That
looks nice. That look real nice."

Jesus said our work is to make the blind see. When the church is
faithful, even those tucked away for years in deep darkness will see that
God is good.

Discussion Questions for Chapter 4
Why Do We Have a Church?

Our Stories
When was the last time you were really proud to be part of a group or community effort? What made that time and those people special?

Reading Review
1. Why do people often define the Church as "full of hypocrites"? How do you see it?

2. How can the Church complete each one of us?

3. What is the real reason we gather with other people to worship God?

Bible Connections
1. Read **John 14:12**. Why do we have a hard time believing Jesus' bold statement about Christians and the Church?

2. Read **Ephesians 5:25-30**. Using an illustration from marriage, how does Paul contend the Church is transformed into goodness?

3. Read **1 Corinthians 12:12-20**. What does Paul call the Church? Does Paul's term ring true for you, or does the Church seem more like an institution to you?

4. Read **Acts 2:41-47**. According to Luke, the author of Acts, what elements characterized that first Christian community? How can we moderns recover some of those qualities?

Chapter 5

Why Do We Pray?

What is prayer?

The most courageous thing my mother ever did was from a lonely place of great pain. Often I have imagined her sitting there in her favorite burgundy chair, occasionally arising from it for no evident reason and with no apparent destination. All the while, she tightly holds a crinkled piece of paper. Every few seconds she opens her fist to look at what is written on the paper, only to tighten her fist around it once more. Mother knew what she must do. For days, perhaps weeks and months, she had known what she must do in order to reclaim her life. The thought of the action she must take left her in utter anguish.

Finally, she opens her fist to look again at the piece of creased, brown paper. She notes the number printed there, even though she had memorized it days before. Propping the receiver between her chin and shoulder, she dials the number. The phone rings six times before it is answered by the weakened voice of an elderly man, "Hello."

"Sir, this is Johnny Gahan's mother, and I am calling to tell you that you did not kill my son. It was raining. It was dark. You couldn't see the lines. You did not kill my son and his wife."

The feeble voice responds, "You don't know how much I needed to hear those words."

"I think I do," she said, "because I know how badly I needed to say them."

It was more than ten years after my brother's death before I heard this story from Mother. Prior to that time, I only knew that at some point Mother returned to herself and to us, her remaining family. Before she made that call, she was in exile from her life. In the still convicting solitude of her home, Mother was moved to make the call, a call that would liberate her from the fear and anger that imprisoned her. She did not profess she received some signal flare from God or some clearly dictated message from the Almighty. I believe she would admit just the opposite. At that pivotal moment in her life when she wavered between an almost physiological need to preserve her anger and a deep spiritual desire to extend forgiveness, it seemed God was shadow-boxing with her. She prayed earnestly and exhaustively, yet God's will seemed indistinct and elusive. Ultimately, she bravely stepped out to offer the man forgiveness, unsure if giving up her hold on anger would heal or destroy her.

Prayer is a courageous act because we cannot dictate God's response to us. We want a secret recipe for prayer, imagining if we get it right, the perfect answers will come to us on a divine ticker tape. Prayer is not a formula, however. It is a relationship – a relationship with One who loves us immeasurably, but Who will not be defined or constrained by us. Paul, who was the first and arguably the best Christian systematic theologian of all time, concluded that even as we come to terms with the vast goodness of God as witnessed through Jesus Christ, humans still come up short in our understanding of God.

Romans 11: 33-36 (The Message)

Have you ever come on anything quite like this
extravagant generosity of God, this deep, deep wisdom?
It's way over our heads. We'll never figure it out.

"Is there anyone around who can explain God?
Anyone smart enough to tell him what to do?
Anyone who has done him such a huge favor
that God has to ask his advice?"

Everything comes from him;
Everything happens through him;
Everything ends up in him.

Therefore, our prayers are woefully inadequate when we make them merely a shopping list of our current desires and demands. Perhaps it is better to think about prayer as a language of love. It may sound outlandish to think of prayer with God, who is beyond human defintion, in terms of romantic language. That is precisely why prayer is a critical element of the Christian life. The language needed to express our communion with God is so unfathomable that ordinary discourse is insufficient.

Furthermore, our life with God is not to be prescriptive but relational. The deepest need of human life is to fall more deeply in love with God. Our romance with God completes us. Regrettably, most of us spend the better part of our lives trying to replace the love only God can give with transitory loves. Augustine, the brilliant fifth century scholar, theologian, orator, and bishop, candidly chronicles in his <u>Confessions</u> the many loves he sought that failed to satisfy him. "I went to Carthage, where I found myself in a hissing cauldron of lust. I had not yet fallen in love but was in love with the idea of it, and this feeling that something was missing made me despise myself for not being more anxious to satisfy the need. I began looking around for some object for my love, since I badly wanted to love something."[12] The central theme of Augustine's autobiography is that our hearts' desire remains unfulfilled until it is opened to the love of God. There is a hole within each of us that can only be filled by God. Augustine warns us from his own life's story that we can look frantically for love other places, but our desperation will only increase. "The god I worshipped was my own delusion, and if I tried to find a place to rest my burden, there was nothing there to uphold it. It only fell and weighed me down once more, so that I was still my own unhappy prisoner."[13] Augustine contends that while we are chasing fleeting loves down dead-end roads,

---

[12] Augustine, <u>Confessions</u> 3:1, trans. R.S. Pine-Coffin, (London: Penquin Books, 1961), 55.
[13] Augustine, <u>Confessions</u> IV: 7, trans. R.S. Pine-Coffin, (London: Penquin Books, 1961), 78.

God is in pursuit of us. The psalmist, much like Augustine, colorfully depicts God as pursuing us vehemently into every imaginable corner of our lives from birth and beyond death.

Psalm 139:7-13 (NRSV)

7 Where can I go from your spirit?
Or where can I flee from your presence?
8 If I ascend to heaven, you are there;
if I make my bed in Sheol (Hell), you are there.
9 If I take the wings of the morning
and settle at the farthest limits of the sea,
10 even there your hand shall lead me,
and your right hand shall hold me fast.
11 If I say, "Surely the darkness shall cover me,
and the light around me become night,"
12 even the darkness is not dark to you;
the night is as bright as the day,
for darkness is as light to you.
13 For it was you who formed my inward parts;
you knit me together in my mother's womb.

Our primary part in prayer is to receive this love freely and generously given by God. Additionally, we know from human experience, the more deeply we love someone, the less we expect to control that person or even want to. Freedom increases in a love relationship. If we could dictate how God answers us in prayer, it would hardly be a relationship. Indeed, it would make God a sort of cosmic vending machine. Prayer begins and is sustained in freedom. God freely chooses to come to us in prayer and we have the freedom to respond to God's romantic advances or not. God is certainly not a vending machine but neither are we marionettes.

My mother, in fact, was free to live with her anger. It was not a good companion, but it was a familiar one. Instead, she chose to open herself and her pain to God. Her choice to lay her need and herself before God was risky. Matters of the heart always are. Mother's response from God did not come like a fierce, distinctive lightening bolt, rather it was delivered softly into the dark solitude of her heart, where she was free to accept or decline the gift.

Thus, the most powerful examples of prayer in the scripture are ones set in the painful darkness of the human situation where rote answers would hardly suffice. Jesus, himself, on the night he realized a friend had betrayed him and his persecution by the authorities was imminent, took three of his remaining friends and began to offer anguished prayers to God.

Matthew 26:37-44 (NRSV)

37 He took with him Peter and the two sons of Zebedee, and began to be grieved and agitated.38 Then he said to them, "I am deeply grieved, even to death; remain here, and stay awake with me."39 And going a little farther, he threw himself on the ground and prayed, "My Father, if it is possible, let this cup pass from me; yet not what I want but what you want."40 Then he came to the disciples and found them sleeping; and he said to Peter, "So, could you not stay awake with me one hour?41 Stay awake and pray that you may not come into the time of trial; the spirit indeed is willing, but the flesh is weak."42 Again he went away for the second time and prayed, "My Father, if this cannot pass unless I drink it, your will be done."43 Again he came and found them sleeping, for their eyes were heavy.44 So leaving them again, he went away and prayed for the third time, saying the same words.

Jesus' prayer in this passage serves as a guide for those of us learning about prayer. First of all, he is in a place of black despair. Yet Jesus is not frantically looking for a list of answers from God or a roadmap of the events to befall him. Very much like my mother alone in her house that day, Jesus suspects his next steps will lead to even greater pain. In his agony, Jesus wants to draw close to the One whom he loves more than any other. He seeks communion with God in his time of sorrow and decision. It is love of God Jesus desires not a divine repairman. Frankly, if we are honest with ourselves, we will admit that not one of our deepest needs can be met by a quick fix. Broken hearts and broken lives cannot be mended by a dose of celestial aspirin, but only through an enduring relationship with the living God.

David, the most celebrated king and warrior in the history of Israel is also its most notable sinner. Confronted by his sins of adultery and murder, David is in his own dark place that he prepared for himself. His greatest fear, however, is not loss of his position or kingdom or reputation. No, his greatest fear is separation from God. David realizes that there is no easy avenue to pull him out of this black hole of his own greed and desire. So he prays that his communion with God will not be erased.

Psalm 51:9-12 (NRSV)

9 Hide your face from my sins,
and blot out all my iniquities.
10 Create in me a clean heart, O God,
and put a new and right spirit within me.
11 Do not cast me away from your presence,
and do not take your holy spirit from me.
12 Restore to me the joy of your salvation,
and sustain in me a willing spirit.

Second, Jesus wishes to be obedient to the will and purpose of God. True, he would like to avert the calamity and pain gathering before him. Jesus is experiencing such personal torture that he throws himself on the ground of the Gethsemane Garden in misery. Nevertheless, he wants to serve the larger purposes of God more than escape his pain. The psalmist sings, "The steadfast love of God is better than life."(63:3) As our own communion with God increases through our life of prayer, so does our determination to abide in God's perfect

will, even if it is a place of pain.
desires have no merit. They d
intercessions to God for ourselve
however, will increasingly overwhe
be in the presence of the Father an

Most often our parade of c
outside of ourselves. We imagine th
shelf out there somewhere or packa
undiscovered. The more we look i
distance increases between us and _____ object of our desire. We
must go inside ourselves to the One who already awaits us there. The
communion we seek and the purpose we desire have been pursuing us
as we have chased other, lesser gods. When Augustine discovered he
had long searched in the wrong places for his true heart's desire, his
deep lament is coupled to that bright discovery: "I learnt to love you
late, Beauty at once so ancient and so new! I have learnt to love you late!
You were within me, and I was in the world outside myself."[14]

Third, Jesus admonishes his three friends to wake up to pray. The
three were invited to be a part of this pivotal movement in Jesus'
suffering and death, which will ultimately be his glorification. To do so
they must become fully awake to God and to themselves. Prayer is an
awakening. We only come to know our true selves through our
communion with the Father who created us. The deep abiding
communion we so desire with others is possible if we open ourselves
fully to God in prayer. We must offer a quiet space for the Holy Spirit
to restore us and make us truly available to others. Henri Nouwen
warns us about the folly of pursuing meaningful relationships with
others in the absence of communion with God: "No friend or lover, no
husband or wife, no community or commune will be able to put to rest
our deepest cravings for unity and wholeness. And by burdening others
with these divine expectations, of which we ourselves are only partially
aware, we might inhibit the expression of free friendship and love and

---

[14] Augustine, <u>Confessions</u> 10:27, trans. R.S. Pine-Coffin, (London: Penquin Books, 1961), 55.

inadequacy and weakness."[15] We are not whole
our personal relationships remain incomplete in
ence.

esus continues to "pray the same words" even in the face
nting despair and his desertion by the disciples. He is certain
Father will be faithful to him. Jesus is confident in the efficacy
is prayer. While he is uncertain where his prayers will lead him, he
s convinced that his ultimate destination will be in God. Prayer is an
athletic exercise. We continue to pray, even when it seems fruitless.
Prayer can never be a purposeless exercise. God is at work in us and in
our situation in ways that may at first elude our understanding. A friend
once told me "grace is only seen in retrospect." In other words, we only
see God at work in our lives on the other side of experience. We
steadily pray in the confidence that God will be faithful. Although
God's fidelity may not be immediately realized, prayer boldly extends us
into the Father's will and mercy. C.S. Lewis, while grieving the death of
his wife, was noted as saying, "Prayer doesn't change God; it changes
me." The most miraculous work of God reorients the stubborn, staid
insides of men and women.

My favorite bible story about persistence in prayer is the account of
the Canaanite woman who entreats Jesus to heal her demon-possessed
daughter. She follows Jesus and his disciples along the dusty roads of
Tyre and Sidon begging for their attention to her desperate need. The
band walks along ignoring her, seemingly for miles. Nevertheless, the
woman's cries will not be silenced. The disciples are aggravated by her
unrelenting pleas, so they urge Jesus to dismiss this pesky foreign
woman. What follows is likely the rudest recounting of Jesus' words to
anyone in the scripture. He tells the woman that she and her daughter
are outsiders, animals in fact, undeserving of God's grace. The
Canaanite woman immediately retorts that she is confident there is
enough bounty on God's table to share well beyond Israel. Jesus,
amazed at her reply, grants her request and heals her daughter.

---

[15] Henri J.M. Nouwen, <u>Reaching Out</u> (Garden City, NY: Doubleday, 1966) 19.

Matthew 15:21-28 (The Message)

From there Jesus took a trip to Tyre and Sidon. They had hardly arrived when a Canaanite woman came down from the hills and pleaded, "Mercy, Master, Son of David! My daughter is cruelly afflicted by an evil spirit."
Jesus ignored her. The disciples came and complained, "Now she's bothering us. Would you please take care of her? She's driving us crazy."
Jesus refused, telling them, "I've got my hands full dealing with the lost sheep of Israel."
Then the woman came back to Jesus, went to her knees and begged. "Master, help me."
He said, "It's not right to take bread out of children's mouths and throw it to dogs."
She was quick: "You're right, Master, but beggar dogs do get scraps from the master's table."
Jesus gave in. "Oh, woman, your faith is something else. What you want is what you get!" Right then her daughter became well.

This story is disturbing on one hand, but quite encouraging on the other. The Canaanite woman had more than sufficient reason to cease her intercessions to Jesus. She was not only ignored but also insulted. Nevertheless, the woman was in a place she never imagined herself – witnessing the unremitting torture of her daughter. She refuses to hold her peace. Her need is too great to be eclipsed by formalities. The woman approaches a rabbi she did not really know who represents a religion she did not yet practice. To pray only when we have developed an airtight understanding of God or a clear avenue of practice will discourage prayer. That is what we learn from the Canaanite woman. We go to God with our incomplete understanding and our unrefined petitions knowing it is the only avenue to healing and wholeness. Prayer is going to the One who loves us and who wants more life for us than we dare want for ourselves.

Matthew 7:7-11 (NRSV)

*7 "Ask, and it will be given you; search, and you will
find; knock, and the door will be opened for you.8 For
everyone who asks receives, and everyone who searches
finds, and for everyone who knocks, the door will be
opened.9 Is there anyone among you who, if your child
asks for bread, will give a stone?10 Or if the child asks
for a fish, will give a snake?11 If you then, who are evil,
know how to give good gifts to your children, how much
more will your Father in heaven give good things to those
who ask him!*

How do we pray?

The hardest part of prayer is beginning and once we have taken
that initial step to tenaciously continue to pray. In fact, the first tenet of
prayer is to develop a habit of prayer, to pray even on those days when
we feel uninspired, disconnected, and lifeless. My own discipline of
prayer began after the untimely death of my brother and his pregnant
wife. The deaths brought down a veil of despair upon me that I deftly
disguised but could not shake. I continued to make my way to work
each day, play with the kids, complete household tasks, and gather with
friends while the unrequited sadness slowly suffocated me. Finally,
Bishop Stough, the bishop of Alabama at that time, detected my
despondency through a conversation we shared, and he arranged for me
to see Ron DelBene, an Episcopal priest, counselor, and author. The
counseling he offered me that year was harder than any preseason
football practices I endured in either high school or college, but at the
end of that time I liked the man I saw in the mirror much more than
the one who first entered Ron's office months before.

Toward the end of our time together, Ron asked me what was the
single most pressing desire of my heart. I immediately answered,
"peace." He said I must construct a simple prayer petitioning God for
the peace I so wanted. Editing out the flowery church words of my
supplication, I came up with a simple, direct prayer: "Lord Jesus, grant

me your peace." Satisfied, Ron instructed me how to reform my intercession into a "breath prayer," similar to the one found in the Russian Orthodox classic The Way of the Pilgrim. He told me to find a quiet place, sit up straight in a wooden chair, place both feet on the floor, open my hands with my palms turned upward, close my eyes, and repeat the sentence with each breath. I was to begin by completing the exercise for ten minutes morning and night, then build up to fifteen, twenty, thirty, and occasionally even an hour at one sitting. According to Ron, the object of the simple prayer exercise was to eventually offer the prayer all day with each breath. In that way, he said, the prayer will become part of your life.

For me, the prayer came to life just as Ron asserted it would. Within a few weeks of keeping the discipline, I seemed to pray the prayer with each breath – even while in meetings, driving the car, enjoying a conversation, or watching TV. What's more, I miraculously began to realize the peace for which I prayed. The dark curtain shrouding my life began to evaporate.

For prayer to have power in our lives, it must escape the limiting bounds of our sparse prayer times and enter our routine experience. Prayer must come to life in our everyday walk. As long as prayer is relegated to the ten minutes we give our formal devotions on those rare mornings and evenings we get around to them, it has no power to change us. We must give God a consistent avenue of transformation within ourselves.

Ironically, for prayer to become more than duty it must become habitual. Prayer is like physical exercise in that way. The benefits of exercise clearly extend well beyond the forty-five minute or so sessions we allow for it. A person thinks more clearly, his mood is enhanced, his diet is more controlled throughout the day, and all those benefits are due to the short time spent sweating in the gym. Making exercise habitual is the key to realizing those positive effects in other aspects of daily life.

Prayer is very much the same – only more so. A prayer-laced life opens us up to the presence and guidance of God in our everyday encounters and trials. While the world shouts conflict at us, the Lord whispers peace. We become like Elijah frantically escaping the bloodthirsty pagan queen Jezebel, who is determined to murder him. Although Elijah is swept up in a storm of fear and hopelessness, God answers his desperate prayer through the silence of his heart.

> 1 Kings 19:11-13

> *11 He said, "Go out and stand on the mountain before the LORD, for the LORD is about to pass by." Now there was a great wind, so strong that it was splitting mountains and breaking rocks in pieces before the LORD, but the LORD was not in the wind; and after the wind an earthquake, but the LORD was not in the earthquake;12 and after the earthquake a fire, but the LORD was not in the fire; and after the fire a sound of sheer silence.13 When Elijah heard it, he wrapped his face in his mantle and went out and stood at the entrance of the cave. Then there came a voice to him that said, "What are you doing here, Elijah?"*

If we make prayer the foremost habit of our daily lives, we will begin to receive the calm assurance of God even in the midst of chaos and pain. Although Elijah is portrayed as a bastion of godly strength and faith only one chapter before, now he doubts an end to his calamity is remotely possible. How incredibly human the great prophet is! We talk and act with confidence until the water starts rising, then we begin to falter. Nevertheless, fortified by a routine of prayer, God will speak through the storm. Brother Lawrence, the 17th century soldier turned monk writes of this strengthening discourse between God and us in his classical text The Practice of the Presence of God: "I do nothing else but abide in his holy presence, and I do this by simple attentiveness and a habitual turning my eyes on him. This I should call...a wordless secret conversation between the soul and God which no longer ends."[16]

---

[16] Brother Lawrence, The Practice of the Presence of God cited by Richard J. Foster, Streams of Living Water (San Francisco: Harper Collins, 1998) 52.

As we progress in our discipline of prayer, we will become more and more like Jesus asleep in the boat that night on the Sea of Galilee. As a storm rages all about him and his disciples, his peace is unassailable. The prayer-laced life is a consistent life, undeterred by the procession of disturbances hurled at each one of us. We do not become numb – far from it. We feel confident in God's presence even to feel deep pain.

Mark 4:34-39 (NRSV)

35 On that day, when evening had come, he said to them, "Let us go across to the other side."36 And leaving the crowd behind, they took him with them in the boat, just as he was. Other boats were with him.37 A great windstorm arose, and the waves beat into the boat, so that the boat was already being swamped.38 But he was in the stern, asleep on the cushion; and they woke him up and said to him, "Teacher, do you not care that we are perishing?"39 He woke up and rebuked the wind, and said to the sea, "Peace! Be still!" Then the wind ceased, and there was a dead calm.

Beyond the storms that come to each one of us, if we develop a routine of prayer, we will not become captive to life's inordinate flow of demands. A regimen of prayer adds a sane, creative rhythm to life unavailable from any other source or activity. The prayer-laced life is one that has meaning regardless of our mundane activities and tasks on a given day. In a tangible way, prayer keeps the fires of adventure alive within each of us. A consistent diet of prayer helps us to experience life as unfolding discovery instead of deadly stagnation and boredom. Prayer becomes the march of everyday life, adding self-discovery and ultimate purpose to what once seemed our pointless, disconnected daily responsibilities. John MacQuarrie, one of the leading Anglican theologians of this generation, describes the power of daily prayer this way:

The problem for the person living under the strains and stress of the everyday world is how to combine order and freedom. How can one have a rule of prayer that will be flexible enough to allow one to meet the incessant and unpredictable demands made upon one's time, and yet firm enough to provide a basis of order that preserves some serenity (or even sanity) and prevents life from degenerating into a meaningless succession of more or less unrelated tasks and enjoyments. How can there be a powerful ordering of time outside the monastery walls when one must also be free for the innumerable demands of family, work, neighbor, civic responsibilities, and all the rest? This is the question which Bonhoeffer faced, using a musical metaphor which is not very far removed from our forgoing discussion about the ordering of life. Bonhoeffer talked about the 'polyphony' of life. What I mean is that God wants us to love him eternally with our whole hearts – not in such a way to weaken or injure our earthly love, but to be a kind of 'cantus firmus' to which other melodies provide the counterpoint. The cantus firmus is the recurring rhythmic pattern which serves as a basis for the music, giving it unity and consistency. Translated into spiritual terms, it is the recurring cycle of prayer and communing with God which gives, as it were, the dominant set to life. But over that cantus firmus all kinds of distinct melodies may be heard interweaving in a complex texture.[17]

Thought of in this way, the outcome of prayer is always miraculous and perhaps even more so than when we witness a particular healing or conversion as a result of praying. Prayer has the power to transform mundane daily life into purposeful eternal life; therefore, prayer is the miracle that consecrates our routine life into a sacrament. The prayer-laced life continuously discloses the divine within what was once considered merely the regimen of meaningless tasks. Our rudimentary lives become transparent symbols to the world that God is at work within humanity. That is a miracle of the first order!

Our prayers must be convicting if they are to miraculously transform us. Therefore, the second tenet of Christian prayer is that our appeals to God must challenge us. Consider for a moment Jesus' answer to his disciples when they asked him how to pray. He responded to

---

[17] John MacQuarrie, <u>Paths in Spirituality,</u> 2nd Edition (Harrisburg, PA: Morehouse Publishing, 1972) 118.

them with a prayer of such sparse, pointed content that it has never ceased to inspire those many who daily use it. In fact, when the Lord's Prayer is considered line by line, it beseeches God to do nothing less than cause revolution within our hearts.

Matthew 6:7-13 (NRSV)

7 "When you are praying, do not heap up empty phrases as the Gentiles do; for they think that they will be heard because of their many words. 8 Do not be like them, for your Father knows what you need before you ask him.
9 "Pray then in this way:
Our Father in heaven,
hallowed be your name.
10 Your kingdom come.
Your will be done,
on earth as it is in heaven.
11 Give us this day our daily bread.
12 And forgive us our debts,
as we also have forgiven our debtors.
13 And do not bring us to the time of trial,
but rescue us from the evil one.

Our internal revolution is not far different from a country in revolt. The old powers must be toppled so that a new power can reign. It is the same way within our hearts, for we must personally be unseated from power before God can take the proper place in our lives. Just writing these lines reminds me of a popular pamphlet used in campus ministries when I was an undergraduate. The pamphlet was an odd-sized, goldenrod colored booklet entitled The Four Spiritual Laws. I cannot recall the entire contents of the small leaflet, but I do remember vividly the opening two pages. The first page depicts a chair set as a sort of cosmic throne in an individual's life and the reader is seated on that throne. On the next page, God has replaced the reader upon the throne, which, of course, is the proper order of things prescribed by

Holy Scripture. In other words, the first order of prayer business is to overthrow the imagined rulers of our cosmos – ourselves.

To pray in such a revolutionary way, takes a great deal of courage because we cannot be certain what God will do with us from that seat of ultimate power in our lives. All of us have certain chambers in our lives that we would like to keep closed, and we can keep them closed as long as we are in charge. An Army friend of mine illuminated this fact for me while the two of us were serving on a lonely military deployment. He confessed that he had prayed for God to clearly show him his daily sin. He added that he was afraid to pray the prayer again because the procession of his petty sins was illuminated for him as if on the big screen of a movie theater. God had been faithful, my friend admitted, but the sordid truths about himself were incredibly painful to confront. Nevertheless, he had radically changed his ways after the prayer projected his sins to him in *Technicolor*. He had become more the person he desired, which is almost always a revolutionary and agonizing process.

Standing in the knee-deep snow along what was then the East German border, my friend taught me just how challenging prayer can be – and should be. We should expect to be challenged and changed by our prayers. If we look closely at the Lord's Prayer, we will note that the petitions address less about those things outside us than it does about our internal lives. Jesus' terse prayer entreats us to courageously open ourselves to radical change. The brilliant second century African church father and scholar, Tertullian of Carthage, reflects on the meaning of the Lord's Prayer in this same way. He notes that we come to God from a position of extreme humility so that "heavenly" work may be accomplished within us:

> When we pray 'thy will be done on earth as it is in
> heaven,' we do not imply that anyone could
> prevent the fulfillment of God' will or that he
> needs our prayer to accomplish his will. Rather, we
> pray that his will be done in all. Think of heaven
> and earth as a picture of our very selves, spirit and
> flesh. The sense of the petition is the same, namely

that in us (as spirit and flesh, as heaven and earth combined) the will of God may be done on earth as it is in heaven. Now, what does God will more than that we ourselves walk according to his ways? We ask therefore that he supply us with the energy of his own will and the capacity to do it, that we may be saved, both in heaven and on earth.[18]

Of all the prayer scenes in the bible, the one that has most fascinated me is the one of Isaiah praying in the Temple. I imagine Isaiah faithfully making his way to his favorite spot in the Temple and then praising and petitioning God in prayer, as he had done many times before. Yet, on this occasion, much like my Army friend, Isaiah is completely unprepared for the response he receives. When God is seated on the throne of our lives, we no longer manage the outcome.

Isaiah 6:1-5 (NRSV)

1 In the year that King Uzziah died, I saw the Lord sitting on a throne, high and lofty; and the hem of his robe filled the temple.2 Seraphs were in attendance above him; each had six wings: with two they covered their faces, and with two they covered their feet, and with two they flew.3 And one called to another and said:
"Holy, holy, holy is the LORD of hosts;
the whole earth is full of his glory."
4 The pivots on the thresholds shook at the voices of those who called, and the house filled with smoke.5 And I said:
"Woe is me! I am lost, for I am a man of unclean lips, and I live among a people of unclean lips; yet my eyes have seen the King, the LORD of hosts!"

---

[18] Tertullian, "On Prayer 4.1-2." <u>Ancient Christian Commentary on Scripture: Matthew</u>, Manlio Simonetti and Thomas C. Oden, eds. (Downers Grove, IL: InterVarsity Press, 2001) 134.

Coming into contact with the Holy God was enough for Isaiah. In the face of the Lord, the prophet is overcome with his own insufficiency and sin. Isaiah seems to undergo the same experience as my friend. His spiritual blemishes and shortcomings are projected to him in immediate, sordid detail in the presence of the One who stands beyond our petty worldliness. He never imagined that God would forgive him and then go on to ask something of him.

Isaiah 6:6-8 (NRSV)

> 6 *Then one of the seraphs flew to me, holding a live coal that had been taken from the altar with a pair of tongs. 7 The seraph touched my mouth with it and said: "Now that this has touched your lips, your guilt has departed and your sin is blotted out." 8 Then I heard the voice of the Lord saying, "Whom shall I send, and who will go for us?" And I said, "Here am I; send me!"*

Isaiah illustrates the third tenet of Christian prayer: authentic prayer requires a response from the believer. When the prophet answers the call, "Whom shall I send?" with "Here am I; send me!" he is humbly inviting the Kingdom of God into his life. Turning again to the text of the Lord's Prayer, when we pray, "Thy kingdom come, Thy will be done on earth as it is in heaven," we are entreating God not only to begin His rule on earth, but also to begin to rule in our hearts. Just like our forerunner Isaiah, when we open up ourselves with prayer, we find God will not be held at a comfortable arm's length. God intends to stoke the tepid coals of our life and turn up the heat within the believer. The Lord will push us out of the comfort zone of our devising just as sure as He pushed Isaiah out the doors of the magnificent Temple that day.

Growing up in the Deep South, I was incessantly jolted out of my comfort by street evangelists, Vacation Bible School teachers, and other neighbors who asked if I had "prayed to invite Jesus into my heart?" In self-defense, I quickly answered yes on every occasion. However, I now know that neither my inquisitors nor I had any inkling how big a question was being asked. They should have asked, "Have you humbly prayed that God will rule your life and turn it and you inside out?" Put that way, I doubt the question would have danced off my neighbors' lips quite so glibly.

Russian Orthodox Archbishop Anthony Bloom, in his modern classic Beginning to Pray, frankly expresses the magnitude of extending such an invitation to God Almighty – hardly an invitation to take lightly. The challenge, according to Archbishop Bloom, is to personally become receptive ground for the reign of God. Our humility before God then becomes an attribute of strength rather than a sign of fearful resignation.

> The word 'humility' comes from the Latin word 'humus' which means fertile ground. To me, humility is not what we often make of it: the sheepish way of trying to imagine that we are the worst of all and trying to convince others that our artificial ways of behaving show that we are aware of that. Humility is the situation of the earth. The earth is always there, always taken for granted, never remembered, always trodden on by everyone, somewhere we cast and pour out all the refuse, all we don't need. It's there, silent and accepting everything and in a miraculous way making out of all the refuse new richness in spite of corruption, transforming corruption itself into a power of life and new possibility of creativeness, open to the sunshine, open to the rain, ready to receive any seed we sow and capable of bringing thirtyfold, sixtyfold, a hundredfold out of every seed.[19]

The archbishop's words cite another challenge realized from the revolution God will stir up in our hearts: the trash of our lives will be refashioned into riches. Those things we once regretted about ourselves or found embarrassing or thought held us back will become the buried treasure on which the kingdom will be planted. Our prayer will not be a plea to

---

[19] Archbishop Anthony Bloom, Beginning to Pray (Ramsey, NJ: Paulist Press, 1970) p. 35.

forget our past but for God to use it. What we once considered the rubbish of our lives will become a gemstone of unrealized personal creativity.

This revolutionary truth became apparent to me during a time of significant growth in a parish I served. We held monthly newcomers' meetings so those many entering our church could receive a more comprehensive welcome, learn about our particular fellowship, and tell some of their own story. Before we invited each attendee to tell their spiritual biography, a very wise associate of mine would firmly state, "Remember, where you've been is as important as where you are now." She did not want people to interpret their past as refuse but rather as treasure God could use to build the Kingdom within their own lives. Our prayer should challenge us to give all of our lives – past and present – to the One who can create something wonderful out of it.

As we become more responsive and open in our prayer life, it becomes less and less a cerebral enterprise. Proceeding from our faith, prayer becomes an act of the whole person, where we extend our selves to God and to both persons we know and do not know. The expression of the prayerful person extends vertically to God, and, at the same time, prayer extends horizontally towards others. It is not merely altruism that directs prayer outward, but a deep need for communion. Prayer is incomplete as a solitary enterprise. Both vertically and horizontally, the person craves reciprocation, a dialogue of sorts, which binds the Christian to God and humanity.

Every time I consider this vertical and horizontal communion Christians seek, I remember my Aunt Florence and her prayers offered for her adult daughter, my cousin Gladys, who was suffering terribly with terminal breast cancer. On Sundays and Wednesdays, my aunt would go to the dark oak altar rail of our old parish church, kneel, and then extend her hands to receive the host (the communion bread). Florence said each time she lifted her hands at the altar, she lifted them in prayer for Gladys. It was a simple, yet a very powerful act offered by my eldest aunt at a time of great sadness in our family. As a result, I never lift my hands at the altar rail that I do not think of the portrait my aunt painted for me. Prayer seeks communion on two planes of reality – heaven and earth.

Actually, when our life of prayer seeks only divine communion, it becomes self-serving and adulterated. Seeking God, while ignoring our brothers and sisters, makes true communion impossible. In fact, in the opening lines of the great prophetic book of Isaiah, God states that he finds it abhorrent that the people lift their hands to pray at the altar of the Temple when they have not lifted a finger for those hurting in the community. Prayer only exercised on the vertical plane is an abomination to God.

Isaiah 1:15-17

15 When you stretch out your hands,
I will hide my eyes from you;
even though you make many prayers,
I will not listen;
your hands are full of blood.
16 Wash yourselves; make yourselves clean;
remove the evil of your doings
from before my eyes;
cease to do evil,
17 learn to do good;
seek justice,
rescue the oppressed,
defend the orphan,
plead for the widow.

So when my mother, in the loneliness of her home, reached down and dialed the phone that day, she was much like her big sister, who in the communion of her church, lifted her hands to heaven at the altar rail. Both were extending themselves fully into the mystery of God, the pain of others, and, ultimately, bravely reaching back into their own pain. Prayer, then, is not for sissies!

Foundationally, prayer is the dialogue of love between God and us. For our prayers to fan the flames of this divine romance, we must become responsive, receptive ground for God's Word to take root. At times, the ground of our hearts becomes parched due to our indifference to others or personal loss we've experienced. During those painfully dry times, which inevitably come to each one of us and when they come we cannot find the words to speak, it is important to remember that we are just one side of the conversation.

Romans 8:26-27 (NRSV)

26 Likewise the Spirit helps us in our weakness; for we do not know how to pray as we ought, but that very Spirit intercedes with sighs too deep for words.27 And God, who searches the heart, knows what is the mind of the Spirit, because the Spirit intercedes for the saints according to the will of God.

Discussion Questions for Chapter 5
Why Do We Pray?

Our Stories

Recall a time when you could not find the words to accurately describe how you felt and what you did or did not do about it.

Reading Review

1. How can forgiveness be a courageous act? How is it related to prayer?

2. Why is prayer more about receiving than anything else?

3. What's an avenue we may take to become persistent in our prayer life?

Bible Connections

1. Read **Matthew 26:36-46**. How is the freedom to pray or not to pray graphically expressed here both by Jesus and his disciples?

2. Read **Matthew 15:21-28**. What does this outsider have to teach us about persistence in prayer?

3. Read **Matthew 6:7-13**. Why is what we call the *Lord's Prayer* really a call for a complete revolution in our hearts?

4. Read **Romans 8:26-27**. According to Paul, what happens if we can't find the words to pray?

Chapter 6

Why Must Christians Exercise Discipline?

Discipline for what?

Chip Crockett was the worst basketball player I ever coached, but I wish I had a player like him every season. That may sound like an outrageous statement coming from a man who for years has coached his high school and middle school basketball teams to win each time they took to the court. With only five players on the court, you cannot hide anyone in competitive basketball; neither can you humor a player or a parent by awarding undeserved playing time. Whoever steps onto the court must be a contributor. To my surprise, Chip Crockett was a contributor in every game of my best varsity basketball season.

I almost let Chip get away, however. Two weeks into what would become that banner season his senior year, Chip requested a private conference with me after practice. "Coach, I'm not good enough to play with these guys," he said. "I'll practice hard with the team every day if you need me to. I'll give them water. I'll carry towels. But don't give me a uniform. I don't expect to play." I knew Chip to be a serious minded young man. He had started at defensive nose guard on the football team the preceding athletic season. Chip looked me straight in the eyes, as he concluded his sincere speech. When he finished, I responded, "That's exactly why you will play, Chip, but when I put you in the game, make something happen. Make one good thing happen to benefit your team, and that will be enough."

Chip left my office like a house afire. He knew that he was not a basketball player, yet he also knew that he could play tough enough to do one positive thing for his team each time he entered a game. That season Chip practiced harder than anyone on that talent-laden team. He pushed himself through tedious fundamental drills and exhausting conditioning exercises as if he were preparing for the NCAA *Final Four* – often asking "to go again" until he perfected the drill or improved his time. Amongst the graceful, angular ball players, Chip's squatty, fire-plug, 5'10" body looked almost alien. From the moment after our conversation that afternoon, he seemed to take no notice of his limitations. In every game, he made a key rebound, a heroic steal, or a clutch free throw.

Once Chip realized he had something to offer his team, he worked feverishly and consistently to give it whenever he was called upon. His role in that record-breaking season was far from glamorous. Some games he played three minutes or less. Regardless, Chip prepared hard in order to offer his gifts within the allotted time he was granted, and no one seemed to derive more joy from those twenty or so basketball games as he did that year.

Both in athletics and faith matters, we call that kind of preparation and work *discipline*. The word sounds restrictive and punitive until we recognize that discipline is really a means to give a gift and perhaps the ability to receive one as well. In fact, discipline's root meaning is "to learn." Giving does not come naturally. We must learn to extend ourselves to others, and that can be hard work. Like Chip, when we realize we have something valuable to give others, we want to be able to deliver it. Also, like Chip, we must become humble in order to receive gifts God and others may have for us. Discipline is therefore the way our lives are worked into fertile, receptive - humble ground (humus = earth), into truly giving and receiving human beings. A modern Christian attorney with a busy practice recently wrote, "Humility is the key that unlocks the universe."[20] If that is so, how do we discipline ourselves to become such receptive ground for God and for others?

---

[20] John McQuiston, II, <u>Always We Begin Again</u> (Harrisburg, PA: Morehouse, 1996), 55.

Receptivity and generosity may not come naturally to us, yet they are foundational to the Christian life. The cornerstone of the New Testament is God's gift of Jesus Christ to a broken world. The gift of Jesus is the oxygen of our faith, and we humbly receive him and then learn how to graciously give our lives away to others. My oldest son rattled me on this score with a radical paradox of our faith only recently. He said, "Remember, Dad, that Jesus' gift was equal for those who crucified him as well as for those who wept at his tomb." In complete opposition to the world's terms, Christians receive grace from the crucified Christ so we may rise to give even to our enemies. Olympic scale discipline will be needed to prepare us to give that much.

Matthew 5:38-44 (NRSV)

38 "You have heard that it was said, 'An eye for an eye and a tooth for a tooth.'39 But I say to you, Do not resist an evildoer. But if anyone strikes you on the right cheek, turn the other also; 40 and if anyone wants to sue you and take your coat, give your cloak as well; 41 and if anyone forces you to go one mile, go also the second mile.42 Give to everyone who begs from you, and do not refuse anyone who wants to borrow from you. 43 "You have heard that it was said, 'You shall love your neighbor and hate your enemy.'44 But I say to you, Love your enemies and pray for those who persecute you.

What does Christian discipline look like?

No person in history understood the necessity of Christian discipline better than the fifth century Italian monk, Benedict of Nursia. Benedict's own prayerful passion for God's service drove him to form a Christian community on the past site of a pagan temple on Monte Cassino. Benedict considered his fledgling prayer community a "school for the Lord's service." What's more, Benedict's time was as calamitous as our own. Barbarous invaders sacked both Rome and the Christian cities of North Africa in his lifetime. His experiment endured that pagan onslaught and legions of different assaults in its sixteen hundred year history, and is thriving in various expressions all over the world. Benedict's discipline for his communities is contained in the Rule of the Master, which gives essential content and direction to people seeking fuller, creative, compassionate lives testamentary of our Christian identity. As St. Paul wrote to the Ephesians, *"I beg you to lead a life worthy of the calling to which you have been called, with all humility and gentleness, with patience, bearing one another in love, making every effort to maintain the unity of the Spirit in the bond of peace."* (Ephesians 4:1-2) Our worthiness in Christ is bound up in our grateful concrete response to his boundless love for us.

The three main pillars or vows of Benedict's Rule are stability, *conversatio,* and obedience. The serious Christian should cleave to these three pillars, regardless of his particular family and occupational situation, in order to bring his life in Christ to its fullest expression. In the absence of the faith community's discipline, Christian life and prayer can become staid, mechanistic, narcissistic, and inauthentic. No doubt, the words "rule," "school," and "monastery," conjure up a plethora of repressive images for most of us. The objective of Benedict's discipline, however, was to free Christians, in order that they may enjoy generous, unbridled communion with God and His people. The Prologue of the Rule states the goal clearly:

> Therefore we intend to establish a school for the
> Lord's service. In drawing up its regulations, we hope
> to set down nothing harsh, nothing burdensome.
> The good of all concerned, however, may prompt us
> to a little strictness in order to amend faults and to
> safeguard love. Do not be daunted immediately by
> fear and run away from the road that leads to
> salvation. It is bound to be narrow at the outset. But
> as we progress in this way of life and in faith, we shall
> run on the path of God's commandments, our hearts
> overflowing with the inexpressible delight of love.
> Never swerving from his instructions, then, but

faithfully observing his teaching
until death, we shall through pa[...]
sufferings of Christ that we may [...]
in his kingdom. Amen.[21]

Benedict's first pillar – *stability* – may s[...]
our own highly mobile culture of the 21st Ce[...]
is to fully commit oneself to a particular com[...] [...]s day,
it meant a monk would remain until death in the monastery he first
entered. Benedict realized Christian maturity was achieved as the monk
rooted himself to a people, place, and purpose and, likewise, turned and
confronted his limitations and the demons that pursued him. Perceived
that way, stability was not intended to be oppressive or punitive; rather,
to remain faithful to a particular community would usher in true
freedom for the monk. The irritating personalities, the tedium of daily
work, the anger, sorrow, and disgust encountered in the monastery
would most certainly be experienced in any other. The monk would
take along his own flaws to the next community as sure as a turtle takes
his shell wherever it goes.

Few of us will become monks and nuns and enter a monastery or
convent for the rest of our lives. In fact, most of us will move several, if
not many, times in our lives just to keep food on the table and the bills
paid. Sadly, we live in the modern world of transfers, downsizing, and
the choice between upward mobility and unemployment. Nevertheless,
all of us have relationships that are central to us – spouses, children,
friends, co-workers, and our parish families. Stability for us is to fully
commit to those relationships – giving and receiving – thereby
becoming receptive ground for God's Word. When we hold back from
full communion with others, we retreat into false intimacies. Without
stability we become nomads in search of transforming love that was
right in front of us all the time.

---

[21] Esther de Waal, <u>Living with Contradiction: an Introduction to Benedictine Spirituality</u> (Harrisburg, PA: Morehouse Publishing, 1989) p. 6.

nedictines have called stability "creative monotony." To live ive life, however, we must become rooted, diligent, even dogged spiritual journey. It is not enough to compose a beautiful picture, m, or song in our head. Eventually, we must sit down at our easel or desk and work. Even more so, it is not enough to romanticize a life of inspiring Christian fellowship and steadfast prayer, for eventually we must get on with it. The composition of a rich Christian life is fixed in tenacious commitment. Stability then is the acknowledgement that the community in which we are set today is our only one. Knowing that, we will extend ourselves fully into a relationship with the people we are given.

A college professor of mine confronted me once on my lack of stability. At the end of a university function, he took me aside and said, "Pat, you make friends easily, but you then leave those friends scattered all about the road behind you." I was stunned by the professor's words. Now thirty years later, I know he did me a favor. "You can't plant your feet in two places" the saying goes. If you try, you will not be present at either place or to anyone. The detritus of relationships is the result of such in-stability.

Some twenty years later, in stark contrast to my college years, I served as a priest in the isolated out-ports communities of Newfoundland. The Newfoundlanders' favorite invitation for fellowship was "Cup o' tea?" – which meant a visit to their home for myriad sweets and scores of tea refills. Each time my wife and I would begin to stand up to conclude our visit, our host would proclaim a second familiar line, "Lot's o' time!" – which meant please don't rush off. The Newfoundlanders were poor and living with immense social and economic uncertainty due to the ecological destruction of the once abundant fishing banks, yet they allowed nothing to displace their communion with others. Outside forces were unraveling their entire way of life, and still they retained their noble Christian expression of life. I was there to minister to them, but I am afraid it was the other way around.

Our personal pursuit of stability ultimately connects us to the life of Christ, whose resolute fidelity to the Father and to his friends drew him to the Cross. Viewed from that angle, the crucifixion is no longer morbid but glorious. Jesus faithful march toward death becomes a sign to us that love overcomes fear. Unflagging commitment to others is the antidote for a meaningless life. Speaking about his own determined commitment, Jesus commends the same inexorable march of life to his disciples:

John 12:24-25 (The Message)

Listen carefully: Unless a grain of wheat is buried in the ground, dead to the world, it is never more than a grain of wheat. But if it is buried, it sprouts and reproduces itself many times over. In the same way, anyone who holds on to life just as it is destroys life. But if you let it go, reckless in your love, you'll have it forever, real and eternal.

Whereas stability is a vow of dogged commitment, the second Benedictine pillar, *conversatio*, is to remain open to fresh conversion to God. The term *conversatio* is listed in the Latin because the exact translation into English is uncertain. Our best semantic stab at Benedict's intention for the word is daily conversion of life. *Conversatio* disciplines us to remain urgent in our Christian pilgrimage. We are to take each day as a singular, glorious gift.

Brian Taylor offers an image illustrating the urgency of *conversatio* in his book Spirituality for Everyday Living: "There is an open grave outside the Chapel of Christ in the Desert Benedictine Monastery right next to two graves where monks are buried. This reminder, both in the *Rule* and at the monastery, is not for the purpose of instilling guilt and fear but to remind us that now is the hour to live the life we are called to live. Now is the time to forsake spiritual death. Now is the time to choose life."[22]

To turn and choose life is very much on my mind as I write these lines. Only this morning, I attended the burial of one of my student's father. He is only a handful of years older than I, and he died suddenly of brain cancer. The sanctuary of his church was filled with people who loved him and his family. The preacher chose as his text a letter the

---

[22] Brian C. Taylor, Spirituality for Everyday Living: An Adaptation of the Rule of St. Benedict (Collegeville, MN: The Liturgical Press, 1989), 21.

man had only recently written to his friends. The message of the letter was stirringly positive and expressed immense gratitude for the life he had lived. The words bespoke the great love he held for his wife, his four children, his grandchildren, his friends, and for all 34 years of his work. The dying man summed up his thoughts by stating, "I would not exchange a single day of my life even for a cure of my illness." Following the sermon, the preacher asked the entire congregation to join in a responsive reading of the man's favorite prayer, the Prayer of Abbot Alban of St. Anselm's Benedictine Abbey:

> *For all You have given: Thank You God.*
> *For all You have withheld: Thank You God.*
> *For all You have withdrawn: Thank You God.*
> *For all You have permitted: Thank You God.*
> *For all You have prevented: Thank You God.*
> *For all You have forgiven me: Thank You God.*
> *For all You have prepared for me: Thank You God.*
> *For the death You have chosen for me: Thank You God.*
> *For the place You are keeping for me: Thank You God.*
> *For having created me to love You for all eternity:*
> *Thank You God, Thank You God, Thank You God.*

I sat there in the pew utterly amazed. I pictured this middle-aged man cut down by cancer in the prime of his life thanking God for his every experience, the good and the bad, believing the sum of all of them were drawing him closer to God. The almost implausible receptivity of *conversatio* is declared in that brave father's life and his adopted Benedictine prayer.

Just as the vow of stability insists the "grass is not greener over there," the vow of *conversatio* extols us not to put off our lives. Christians are to live fully in the present, which should leave us both expectant and discomfited. On one hand, we should maintain an exuberance of life, expecting the riches each day brings. On the other, however, it is the acceptance of a life of continual growth. No Christian qualifies for cosmic retirement. We should expect the daily pain that spiritual growth and challenge bring to us and expect to continue growing spiritually even after our physical death. God will never be finished making more of us. The resurrection is evidence of the never-ending dynamic life God has in store for us. Coasting to the finish-line is not an option for the disciplined Christian. *"Be dressed for action and have your lamps lit, like those who are waiting for their master to return from the wedding banquet, so that they may open the door for him as soon as he comes and knocks.* (Luke 12:35-36, NRSV)

Benedict seemed to know that the true freedom we desire accompanies a life of growth and challenge. Unbridled license with no commitments is a recipe for a captive life, not a free one. Direction adds meaning to our lives rather than the absence of it. Therefore, the third pillar of the disciplined Christian life is obedience. In Benedict's monasteries, a monk was to obey the abbot of his particular house as if the abbot were Christ himself. The vow of obedience was to benefit the monk and not the abbot, who was chosen for his noted wisdom, godliness, and humility. The abbot would be the least likely one in the monastery who needed the fealty of others, but he would be the most likely one to give beneficial spiritual and temporal direction. Under the leadership of a devoted abbot, a monastery was not a haven of rest but an ordered community constantly challenging its members.

Again, as with the other pillars of Christian discipline, we must translate obedience for life outside Benedict's 6th Century communities. A good starting point for our modern understanding is that obedience is to live for something greater than self – to put ourselves under authority. Of course, we Christians profess the authority of God as revealed in Jesus Christ, yet that submission trips off the tongue easier than it enters our lives. How is our discipline of obedience realized in the day to day? A good starting point is the admission that our life in Christ requires the whole person, the mental, physical, and spiritual parts of ourselves. So while careful study of the Bible, for instance, is important, it is incomplete obedience unless our bodies are subject to Christ's rule as well. Fasting is of great value in Christian formation, but becomes nothing more than pious gymnastics without the assent of the spirit. Prayer is the central expression of the Christian, yet unaccompanied by our faculty of reason leaves no avenue to obey God. Our destination in Christ is to be fully free not just having appendages of ourselves free. The comprehensive nature of Christian obedience requires strenuous compliance. Paul likens our obedience to the training required of an athlete in order to be a champion.

Philippians 3:13-16 (NRSV)

13 Beloved, I do not consider that I have made it my own; but this one thing I do: forgetting what lies behind and straining forward to what lies ahead, 14 I press on toward the goal for the prize of the heavenly call of God in Christ Jesus. 15 Let those of us then who are mature be of the same mind; and if you think differently about anything, this too God will reveal to you. 16 Only let us hold fast to what we have attained.

Simply stated, Christ wants all of us and for all time. No stone may remain unturned in our lives if we wish to experience the incredible freedom Christ offers. Accompanying that freedom will be the birth of meaning and unexpected creativity within us. Don't be misled; however, the birth of this new life in Christ will be painful at times. I can compare it to the trauma of our students at the school I serve after we hired a new art teacher last fall. The students' warm welcome of her quickly soured when she began to teach them. She demanded careful attention to detail, the use of classical methods, and the creation of a mixed-media portfolio. Such was the indignation of the students; they beseeched the Academic Dean and the Headmaster to intervene on their behalf.

Within weeks of her arrival, however, the cries for her removal were replaced by the same students' laudatory exclamations. They stared in disbelief at the art they had produced. While it was true they never expected to work so hard in an art class, neither could they imagine they could create such beauty. Artistic growth is mostly persistent hard work and not spontaneous inspiration.

In the same way, obedience is the laboratory for a beautiful life. Strenuous submission to Christ in every area of our lives will transform us into the art of God's intention. To forego this discipline is to remain incomplete and less productive than we were initially fashioned to be. Christ himself made no secret of his own obedience to the Father. Rather than leave his followers with the illusion that he was simply a clever rabbi with a unique interpretation of the scriptures, he continually professed his fidelity to God. Confronting his critics, Jesus testified: *When you have lifted up the Son of Man, then you will realize that I am he, and that I do nothing on my own, but I speak these things as the Father instructed me. As the one who sent me is with me; he has not left me alone, for I always do what is pleasing to him.* (JN 8:28-29)

Jesus' call to radical obedience was unsettling for those who followed him as well as those who opposed him. With the exception of the despised tax collector Matthew, it is likely that Jesus called each of his disciples away from work and home that had been their family's way of life for generations. Each man was called away from what he knew and prized, and Jesus gave no quarter to personal regret. More than the other three Gospel accounts, Mark centers on the hot and cold responses of Jesus' disciples. Jesus issues the simple invitation of "Follow me," and James, John, Andrew, and Peter get up and leave their families, fishing boats, and home. (MK 1:16-20) Nevertheless, when Peter seeks sympathy or praise for his loyalty to Jesus, he is upbraided:

Mark 10:28-31 (NRSV)

28 Peter began to say to him, "Look, we have left everything and followed you."29 Jesus said, "Truly I tell you, there is no one who has left house or brothers or sisters or mother or father or children or fields, for my sake and for the sake of the good news, 30 who will not receive a hundredfold now in this age—houses, brothers and sisters, mothers and children, and fields, with persecutions—and in the age to come eternal life.31 But many who are first will be last, and the last will be first."

I like English theologian N.T. Wright's take on Mark's call stories. He states, "The way Mark tells the story sends echoes ringing back through the scriptures, the larger narrative of God's people. 'Leave your country and your father's house,' said God to Abraham, 'and go to a land I will show you.' Abraham, like Peter and the others, did what he was told, and he went to where he was sent. Mark was hinting to his readers that the old family business of the people of God is being left behind. God wants a new poetry to be written, and is calling new people to write it."[23]

We undertake the three-fold Christian discipline in order to relinquish our old, stale, uncreative lives. To heed the call of Christ is to be fashioned into his new "poet." As Mother Teresa stated, "Each one of us is to do something beautiful for God." Yoked to the Benedictine disciplines of *stability*, *conversatio*, and *obedience*, we will cease imagining that we are not going anywhere - that our lives are of no account. *Stability* grounds us. *Conversatio* opens us. *Obedience* directs us. We count because we live in communion with God and we are allowing God to form us from the inside out. The fruit of our formation is the ability to give of ourselves and receive from God and those God puts in our paths. The cadences of our new poetry will pulsate in a world deadened by greed, fear, and isolation.

How do we discipline our days?

Any poet will tell you that ideas come easy; the hard part is getting the words on paper. The same is true with athletics. One of my coaches, in his ever-colorful jargon stated, "Every jackass wants to win on game day!" Sure, when we've donned the uniform, and the fans are cheering, and our opponents are looking us up and down – it's easy to be inspired. Only then it is too late. Another coach quipped, "The desire to win must become the discipline to practice." Anything worthwhile we pursue requires the sweat of preparation. Why would we imagine the most important part of our lives – our faith walk – would be any different? In fact, our daily Christian discipline will demand our best

---

[23] N.T. Wright, <u>Mark for Everyone</u> (London: SPCK, 2001), 8.

efforts, day in and day out. True, we are saved by faith in Jesus Christ, but we are not zapped into perfection. We must, as Benedict prescribed, "school" ourselves in the Lord's service.

Benedict determined the monk's day to be comprised of three essential parts: *Opus Dei* – worship, *Lectio Divinia* – spiritual reading or study, and *Labor Manuum* – manual work. In essence, Benedict saw the three legs of daily discipline making up a life of prayer, which is the goal of a monk. Left to our own devices, we quickly allow our lives to become unbalanced, forsaking one essential part of our day for another. For most of us, worship is the first thing to go with physical exercise a close second. Others of us can consume ourselves with the physical, and still others with spiritual matters. Regardless, we can quickly retreat into a one-dimensional existence. For a God who wants all of us, the single-faceted life will not suffice, and the single-faceted Christian who wishes to make her life one of prayerful communion will constantly feel inadequate. Yet Jesus was quite clear that life in union with him was to be a full life, one that would complete us. *I came that they may have and enjoy life, and have it in abundance – to the full, till it overflows.* (John 10:10, Amplified Bible) Paul Tillich wrote of the integrated Christian existence as a complete life and one replete with meaning:

> In the act of faith every nerve of a man's body, every striving of a man's soul, every function of a man's spirit participates. But body, soul, spirit are not three parts of man. They are dimensions of man's being, always within each other; for man is a unity and not composed of parts. Faith, therefore, is not a matter of the mind in isolation, or of the soul in contrast to mind and body, or of the body, but is the centered movement of the whole personality toward something of ultimate meaning and significance.[24]

---

[24] Paul Tillich, <u>Dynamics of Faith</u> (New York: Harper Collins, 1957), 123.

Benedict's *Opus Dei* stakes claim to that integrated life of meaning. Rather than only signifying that part of the day we set aside for communal and private prayers, the *Opus Dei*, "God's Work," is the glue that holds the Christian's entire day together. Our daily existence of prayer, work, play, study, and rest are of one fabric. All that we do are part of the *Opus Dei* and reflects the unified being of faith. So if we are at our desk, driving the company truck, washing the dishes at home, helping our daughter with homework, cooking out on the grill in the backyard, cutting the grass, playing tennis, studying the Bible, or reading a new biography – our efforts are part of the *Opus Dei*. The whole person claims the entire day as a unity directed toward serving God and the people God places into our lives. The goal of the Benedictine Christian is to make the entire day a prayer to God. A Cistercian Benedictine monastery situated just an hour from my home states this desire and effort for an integrated day on their computer website:

> The monk lives for God, in Christ, in the Church,
> by doing things common to the entire human
> family. Monastic life is an attempt to recognize
> consciously how our human existence discloses the
> saving work of Christ and has been encompassed
> by Him. It is a growth in purity of heart toward
> freedom for full conformity to God's will in the
> monk's life: to be re-formed into the likeness of
> God's Son, the Lord Jesus. In this it is no different
> from any committed Christian life. [25]

Regardless of our own similarities with monastic Christians, constructing our days to be part of a unified whole, it seems, requires almost Herculean discipline. Our days are fragmented into stress-charged pieces. By the time we walk out the door in the morning, we often already feel pulled apart by the business and family commitments ahead of us. Add to that stress encountered at the beginning of the day, workplace cultures that can drain civility and reflection from most every

---

[25] Holy Cross Abbey Homepage, www.holycrossabbeybrryvlle.org, p.2

endeavor, children who seem to have as many appointments as their parents, civic responsibilities that feel as antiseptic as our business ones, and before long our car radio may be our most serene companion. At the end of the day, we fall into bed craving the oblivion of sleep.

Given our daily challenges, it appears the *Opus Dei* may be attained in the monastery or convent but not in the schedules we are keeping. The key, however, to unifying our days is to first allow our worn-out vision of what God wants from us to die and then die to our old selfish, ego-driven outlooks. In a very real sense, our days will then be converted because our vision of what constitutes a Godly day will be converted. Few people can speak with more authority on this subject than Jean Vanier, the philosophy professor who took two mentally retarded men into his house in 1964 and subsequently started a movement known worldwide as *L'Arche*, "the Ark", which now numbers over 100 communities of retarded and fully functioning persons living together in caring communities of equality. Vanier states clearly the double conversion that must take place within the Christian in order to re-claim the day:

> More and more people are becoming conscious
> that our God is not just a powerful Lord telling us
> to obey or be punished but our God is family. Our
> God is three persons in love with each other, our
> God is communion. And this beautiful and loving
> God is calling us humans into this life of love. We
> are not alone; we are called together to drop
> barriers, to become vulnerable, to become one. The
> greatest thirst of God is that 'they may become one,
> perfectly one, totally one.' But we have to die to all
> the powers of egoism in ourselves in order to be
> reborn for this new and deeper unity where our
> uniqueness and personal gifts and creativity are not
> crushed but enlivened and enhanced.[26]

---

[26] Jean Vanier, <u>From Brokenness to Community</u> (New York: Paulist Press, 1992), 35.

In a sense, this double conversion is a rebirth into the wonder of the present. Our biggest waste of time may very well be our regret of the past and yearning for the future, and both remain abstractions. They can never be real. I remember yet another time when my mother caught me up short on this very subject. I was a high school English teacher and coach when our first two children were quite young. On this particular weekend, my wife, a registered nurse, was serving at the hospital, and I was left at home with Clay, who was four years old, and Catherine who was six months. Sitting atop the dining room table of our apartment were 135 essays I needed to grade before Monday morning. Yet every time I took out my red pen and sat down to grade, Clay pulled on my arm to come play with him and Catherine cried out for attention as only a six-month old can do. Almost crazed with anxiety, I called my mother for support. She listened to my complaint and then curtly responded, "Pat, when you watch kids, watch kids." Her reply, of course, angered me, but she was absolutely right: if you are watching children, you need to do just that and expect to do little else unless they are napping. Looking back, with Clay now 25 and Catherine 21, how I wish both were still pulling on my arm. My mother and Benedict both knew the present is precious and fleeting. Christians must discipline ourselves to revel in every moment of the day we have and the people and opportunities contained in that day.

Jesus once responded as curtly to one of his dear friends as my mother did to me on the phone that day. The Gospel infers that Jesus visited his friend's Lazarus's home quite often for fellowship and rest. Jesus seemed particularly bound to Lazarus and his two sisters Martha and Mary. On one given visit, Martha was scurrying about preparing the meal for them, while Mary continued to visit with their guest Jesus. Indignant at her sister's supposed sloth, Martha asks Jesus to admonish her sister.

Luke 10:38-42

38 Now as they went on their way, he entered a certain village, where a woman named Martha welcomed him into her home.39 She had a sister named Mary, who sat at

*the Lord's feet and listened to what he was saying.40 But
Martha was distracted by her many tasks; so she came to
him and asked, "Lord, do you not care that my sister has
left me to do all the work by myself? Tell her then to help
me."41 But the Lord answered her, "Martha, Martha,
you are worried and distracted by many things; 42 there is
need of only one thing. Mary has chosen the better part,
which will not be taken away from her."*

It would be wrong to suppose that Martha's preparation of the meal
was less important than Mary's communion with Jesus. If we read closely,
we will see that it is Martha who welcomes Jesus into their household in
the first place (38). Sharing a meal together, especially in the ancient world,
was considered a holy activity. Martha's work was both important and
sacred, as long as she did not fret over her sister's situation and was fully
present to her own duty. Note, however, that Martha was "distracted by her
many tasks", not enrapt by them. Mary on the other hand, had chosen to
avail herself of Jesus' company. Martha is like that young father tucked
away with his two children. Concrete joy was within arm's length, but both
grasped at the straws of abstraction.

Responding to what he saw as the abstract nature of past and
future times, C.S. Lewis wrote, "In a word, the Future is, of all things,
the thing least like eternity. It is the most completely temporal part of
time – for the Past is frozen and no longer flows, and the Present is lit
up with eternal rays."[27] To truly be alight with Christ, we must give
ourselves over to the present, to real experience. We must not allow our
lives to be hid away in nostalgic regret or whimsical longing. It is very
important here to remember that Jesus Christ entered real human time.
Jesus maintained urgency about the present. *"Can any of you by worrying
add a single hour to your span of life? If then you are not able to do so small a
thing as that, why do you worry about the rest?"* (Luke 12:25-26)

In recent years, I have been heavily influenced by time management
guru Stephen Covey of The Seven Habits of Highly Successful People

---

[27] C.S. Lewis, The Screwtape Letters (New York: Harper Collins, 1942), 76.

fame. His constant mantra to his readers is that we do not plan and do the things that matter most. You would think he was mainly talking about business endeavors; however, he focuses most on neglect of our essential relationships due to our poor planning. We allow whole days to go by without attending to the people and things most dear to us. Once I bought into Covey's guidance, I began to write things in my calendar like "letter to Clay", "take Kay to lunch", and "put note in Catherine's lunch bag". Also appearing on my daily calendar were notations stating "exercise", "pray", and "write". In short, I began to take hold of the present, and, on most days, I noticed a measurable difference in my spiritual temperature and family relationships. Among other things, it is a rare week that I fail to write my mother and my three children (if they are away from home), spend significant time with my wife, and pray each day, along with reading four pieces of scripture each morning or evening. I have begun to write everything on my calendar in order to keep some personal accountability.

My days are full – much like yours I bet. What I like about my days, though, is that I really feel them. Certainly, I have a plethora of interruptions like any working person with a big family, but I do live into most days and generally I write a letter or accomplish some enduring thing – even if it is a small one. And even when I am distracted or worried, I seem to maintain a prayer life. It has not always been that way, and while I am not the poster-child for personal piety, discipline has given me back my days. And some of those days have even seemed like prayers themselves.

I have always been particularly convicted by C.S. Lewis's imaginary devil Screwtape who reported the words of a hapless man on his initial arrival in Hell: "I now see that I spent most of my life in doing neither what I ought nor what I liked."[28] We were made for better things.

---

[28] C.S. Lewis, The Screwtape Letters (New York: Harper Collins, 1942), 60.

Discussion Questions for Chapter 6
Why Must Christians Exercise Discipline?

Our Stories

Remember the last time you had to knuckle down and get some work done, get in shape, lose some weight, or make some tough changes.

Reading Review

1. If receptivity and generosity do not come naturally to most of us, what must we do?

2. Why is *stability* a foreign concept to most of us moderns? Why is *stability* foundational to Benedict's rule?

3. How has *obedience* become a dirty word for many of us? How did Benedict see it differently?

Bible Connections

1. Read **John 12:24-25**. Why is this idea of *dying* such a hard pill to swallow? What do these words from Jesus have to say about the *grass always being greener on the other side?*

2. Read **Luke 12:35-36**. Why does Jesus contend that the Christian life should be dynamic from start to finish?

3. Read **John 8:28-29**. How is Jesus our model of *obedience?*

4. Read **Ephesians 4:1-6** and then read **John 10:10**. Why does Paul in Ephesians say we should discipline ourselves? According to Jesus, what is the end result of our disciplined life?

Chapter 7

Why Read the Bible?

What's in the Bible for me?

Without a doubt, my favorite teacher was Mrs. Trawick. She was my second grade teacher at Edgewood Elementary, and the gift she gave me has been almost magical in my life. Although, quite honestly, I cannot remember a single skill she taught me about arithmetic, handwriting, spelling, or coloring within the lines. I cannot recall one moment of our class at recess or the names of my classmates who played beside me there. What I do remember is our class ritual every day after lunch. We would silently file into our musty room on the second floor, satisfied and a little drowsy from our luncheon of peanut butter and jelly sandwiches, potato sticks, and cartons of whole milk. Mrs. Trawick would then move her chair from its customary place behind her desk to directly in front of it. In her hand she held a tattered brown volume. She would sit erectly on the maple-stained chair in her black woolen skirt and her snow white sweater draped on her shoulders with the top button neatly fastened at the neck. Then, without introduction, she would open the book adjust her glasses, and begin to read, transporting me to that wondrous place stored in my imagination from the day before. In the first half of the school year, she read us Tom Sawyer, and when I could not imagine a story better than Tom's, she read us every line of Huckleberry Finn during the second semester. By May, Huck replaced *The Lone Ranger* as my ultimate hero.

Mrs. Trawick allowed us to put our heads on the desks for a nap if we desired. Not me, I would sit up each afternoon exhilarated as if I were atop that raft coursing along the muddy Mississippi with Huck and Jim. I can remember laughing out loud at the antics of the King and the Duke and then groan with disgust when they betrayed my two friends. I cried when Jim was discovered as a runaway slave, and I think I cried over the discovery of slavery itself. I couldn't believe Huck would dress up like a girl or that Tom actually liked girls. Huck's hard-drinking, mean-as-Hell dad did not shock me like he did my classmates, as I was beginning to discover my own dad would get just as drunk and twice as mean. Huck became my secret companion of sorts.

Mostly, Mrs. Trawick and Mark Twain took me to destinations both inside and outside myself I did not think possible, but O how I loved the travel! I got my first library card that summer and rebuffed the entreaties of the librarian and my mother to select books from the *Beginning Readers* section. I wanted to accompany *Horatio Hornblower, the Hardy Boys, Doc Savage*, and Jack London's indomitable dogs on their heroic treks. Since my second grade year with Mrs. Trawick, I have never stopped reading and imagining, and neither have I ceased haunting libraries and bookstores.

That same quest for adventure, introspection, and companionship has drawn me into a lifelong relationship with the Bible, too. I say a "relationship" because I rarely have used the Bible primarily as a reference tool, text book, science, or history volume. For me, it has remained an adventure book – whose characters have more in common with Huck and Jim on the beguiling, yet dangerous Mississippi than with stony-faced preachers pacing across the TV screen wielding the Bible like a club. John Chrysostom, the crusty fourth century Bishop, used his own powerful image of water when preaching on the adventure of reading the Bible to his flock in Constantinople:

> Listen carefully to me, I entreat you...Procure books
> that will be medicines of the soul...At least get a
> copy of the New Testament, the Apostle's (Paul)
> epistles, the Acts, the Gospels, for your constant

teachers. If you encounter grief, dive into them as into a chest of medicines; take from them comfort for your trouble, whether it be loss, or death, or bereavement over the loss of relations. Don't simply dive into them. Swim in them. Keep them constantly in your mind.[29]

Today, in fact, I began the day with such a Biblical adventure. Two of the daily readings assigned from the Book of Common Prayer were from 1 Samuel 3 and Acts 2. In the first reading, Samuel is a boy serving the aged priest Eli. It is night, and both have gone to bed; however, young Samuel is awaked by someone calling his name. Immediately, he goes to the bedside of Eli and asks, "You called, my Lord?" Eli responds that he did not call the boy and for him to go back to sleep. Again, once he gets settled, Samuel hears his name clearly called, and he obediently goes to Eli's side. Eli, perhaps a little huffier this time, states he did not call the boy and for both of them to get back to sleep. No sooner than the boy reclines, he once more hears his name being called. He returns to Eli, and now the aged priest realizes the boy is being sought by God. So, he tells Samuel next time he hears his voice to respond, "Here am I, Lord." The boy does as he is instructed and God shares with him some pretty tough news.

In the second reading from the Acts of the Apostles, the author succinctly reports on the very first days of the newly formed Church. Christ has ascended into Heaven to the Father, the mysterious and unsettling events of Pentecost have just occurred, and now those brave few who first believe that Jesus is the Messiah step out to act on their faith. What do they do? They sell their possessions, live as total equals in community, give to those in great needs, pray daily in the Temple, and break bread together in their homes.

I have read both of these Bible stories numerous times, yet today they grabbed me in a particular way. God speaks to unsuspecting Samuel. He is told by his mentor to make himself available to God and listen. I am convicted by Eli's instructions. Perhaps God has been trying to speak to

---

[29] John Crysostom, Homilies of Colossians, as cited by Christopher A. Hall, Reading Scripture with the Church Fathers (Downers Grove, IL: Inter Varsity Press, 1998), 96.

me, but I have been too busy with frenetic, self-consumed living to hear God, much less respond. It is also possible God is speaking to people I consider unlikely recipients – those who disagree with me, those who hold opinions much different from my own about our Christian faith, and maybe even those I consider far junior to me in the Church.

The story from Acts humbles me as well because I know the rest of the story. The Church began with those few responding in radical obedience. The result was almost incalculable growth of the Christian Church around the Mediterranean in the first and second centuries. At a time when my own denominational church, along with most others is declining in numbers, and we are using one sophisticated strategy after another to stop the bleeding, the earliest Church simply disassembled the common barriers that have forever separated us and prayed, ate, and gave as a community. Do we think we're now above that? More importantly, do I smugly imagine I have transcended the obedience of that first Christian community?

See, the Bible is not tame and it is certainly not boring. It is every bit as wild and dangerous as the wide, muddy Mississippi River transporting my life-long friends Huck and Jim. Just so, the Bible transports all of us Christians on our invigorating and perilous journey. Our trek begins each time we respond to the radical words of that ancient book.

We consider the Church badly fractured with our many distinct denominations and fellowships. However, during my first year of seminary, our Old Testament professor challenged us to imagine we were aliens from another planet investigating the planet Earth and the behavior of its human inhabitants. Among other things, the aliens begin to investigate the Church in its myriad expressions all over the globe. The aliens, my professor noted, found only one thing in common in each place of worship: the public reading of the Bible. Not only does the Holy Scripture contain the familiar stories of our Christian faith, but the book itself is a living symbol of our common life in Christ. Like the vast Mississippi River for Huck and Jim, the Bible is the golden thread connecting all Christians from this generation and with generations long past.

I am writing these lines from the air of all places. I am in route to Austin, TX to bury a former student of mine. He was 25 years old and attending medical school at his death. He was also one of my oldest son's dearest friends since middle school. This will be a tough trip. The boy's parents are devastated and moving deeper and deeper into sorrow as the realization fully consumes them. I am again in that familiar place of feeling unequal to the task before me. From the burial service in the Episcopal Book of Common Prayer, I asked them to choose what Bible readings they would like read at their son's funeral. They chose selections from Lamentations 3, John 10, and the familiar 23rd Psalm. I estimate that I have presided at 700 to 1,000 burials. Thus I have read these prescribed passages many times. Regardless, I eagerly reached for my dog-eared Bible this morning, hoping the words would come alive to me again, as they have faithfully done each time in the past.

Lamentations, a book of five moving poems written after the Babylonian army destroyed Jerusalem and the Temple in 586 B.C., states the "steadfast love of God never ceases" (3:22). I recalled the Hebrew translation of the passage – hesed is the Hebrew word for "steadfast love." In essence, it is the unassailable, unrelenting, imperishable love God has for us, even in our darkest hour. It is hesed that drew Israel out from their Egyptian captors and again, much later, brought them out of their bondage in Babylon. It is the love that loves us even when we are broken or unlovable.

The gospel passage from John, while written 700 years after Lamentations, extends much the same message: Jesus is the Good Shepherd who knows his people and they know him because of his steady care and love for them. In fact, he loves them so much that he gives his own life that we might find ours. Furthermore, he is always looking for more "sheep", for each one of us who has lost our way.

Of course, the best known of the three selections is the 23rd Psalm. I presume it has been read at over three-quarters of all the funerals I have led. It's message resonates with the lines of Lamentations 3 and John 10, yet the psalmist goes further in his attestation: "Lo, though I walk through the valley of the shadow of death, I will fear no evil; for you are with me..."(4) There is no place where we can hide from God's love. Not even death will hide us from the One for whom we are beloved.

So, while I did not have the words to say to this grieving mother and father and the scores of friends and family who will be present, I do have some now. I am amazed every time the Bible speaks to me that way. But I shouldn't be. God uses that adventure book just as deliberately as He spoke to the boy Samuel and to that fledgling band of first Christians. In effect, it is a river of life for us.

I must add, though, that the river of the Bible has unpredictable currents. We may traverse the same route many times, but the stream will pull us a slightly different way each time we enter it. Sometimes I think of the Bible as one of those cleverly constructed children's books that offers multiple conclusions. The reader can wind up with different adventures stemming from the same narrative. When I have allowed myself to honestly enter the Biblical stories, they have often affected me in varied and powerful ways.

How do I read the Bible?

How unfortunate that many people avoid the adventure of the Bible. They have their reasons. For some, the Bible is intimidating. There is just too much disparate material contained in that fat leather-bound book. Some of us have been put off by use of the Bible to support irrational ideas of science, history, or other intellectual notions. For others, the Bible is tedious, replete with cumbersome lists, impractical injunctions, and nonsensical stories. Finally, others have been injured by someone wielding the Bible as a weapon, stressing a point with the knife-edge of a scripture verse. I will attempt to broadly address these unfortunate encounters with the Bible.

First, the Bible is filled with a smorgasbord of literature. There is poetry, legal documents, axioms, prophecies, letters, and songs, among other things. It means not every page of the Bible can be read the same way. A good place to start is to think of the Bible, not as a book, but as a library. Quite literally, the Bible is a collection of books, a library of books in one volume (from Greek *biblia* = books). A book of mine that resembles the Bible is my <u>Norton Anthology of English Literature</u>, which I used exhaustively during my undergraduate studies. Within the anthology are short stories, poems, essays, plays, and even short novels written by a league of authors over a considerable span of time. Only a fool would read each selection in the anthology with its diverse literary genres, different authors, and various periods of English history the same way. We must read the myriad selections in the Bible with a similar sensitivity.

For example, I teach the book of Job to my senior theology students each fall. All but three chapters of Job is an ancient epic poem whose origin predates the Hebrew people. With Job's cast of a furious protagonist, cynical friends, and a somewhat "testy" God, it is unwise to read its pages the same way we would read – let's say – the Gospel of John. Nevertheless, there is much truth and great power in Job. The universal human predicament and the incomparable majesty of God are illustrated candidly by Job if we pay attention to just what we're reading instead of trying to make the poem something it is not. If we are bold enough to read Job that way, we'll see he is asking the questions we've been dying to ask ourselves.

Job 23:1-5 (The Message)

Job said:
'I'm not letting up – I'm standing my ground.
    My complaint is legitimate.
God has no right to treat me like this –
    It isn't fair!
If I knew where on earth to find him,
    I'd go straight to him.
I'd lay my case before him face-to-face,
    Give him all my arguments first hand.
I'd find out exactly what he's thinking,
    Discover what's going on in his head.

Also, I dare to teach the entire book of Revelation every spring to my students. Along with most of Daniel and smaller portions of the Gospels, John's Revelation is *apocalyptic* literature, a narrative constructed to unveil deep truths through cryptic stories and highly symbolic language. To mistake Revelation - with its strange beasts, animated constellations, and array of heavenly beings - for a collection of literal historical predictions, is to dwarf the book. The apocalypse, by design, is neither bound by temporal time or realistic beings. Revelation, much like Job, illustrates powerful truths in humanity's spiritual drama if read in such a way to receive the full force of their power.

Revelation 4:6b-8 (NRSV)

Around the throne, and on each side of the throne, are
four living creatures, full of eyes in front and behind: the
first living creature is like a lion, the second living
creature like an ox, the third living creature with a face
like a human face, and the fourth living creature like a
flying eagle. And the four living creatures, each of them
with six wings, are full of eyes all around and inside. Day
and night without ceasing they sing,
*   'Holy, holy, holy,*
the Lord God the Almighty
*   who was and is and is to come.'*

Curiously, a book I teach each year and have taught more than any other is Galatians. Unlike the strange genres employed by the mysterious authors of Job and Revelation, Galatians is a brutally direct letter unmistakably composed by the apostle Paul to a specific audience regarding some very explicit issues. In a nutshell, the leaders of the Galatian congregation imposed a series of rigid entrance requirements for people seeking membership in the Church. The path to become a Christian took on the appearance of a modern college fraternity initiation with its many "hoops to jump through" to prove the candidates were serious. You can almost hear Paul clearly scream between the lines in the letter. This book of the Bible is anything but veiled and cryptic in content. Paul "pulls no punches" in his letter as he tries to correct the serious detour taken by the Galatian church leaders: *Why don't these agitators, obsessive as they are about circumcision, go all the way and castrate themselves!* (Galatians 5:12, The Message)

So, if the first rule of Bible reading is: *Know what you are reading.* The second is: *Respect what you are reading.* The Holy Scripture is not a product of the 21st Century. The worldview of the Bible is significantly different from our own. Notably, the Old Testament composed in Hebrew during the First Millennium B.C. (or B.C.E. – *Before the Common Era*) depicts a three-tiered universe. That is, the visible sky above is the first tier and the heavenly abode of God, the flat earth – the second tier - is the habitation of humans and other transient life, and finally the third tier is the underworld abode of the dead. The New Testament was written in Greek over a much shorter period of time during the First Century A.D. (C.E.) and reveals a Ptolemaic cosmological view, a round earth situated in the center of the solar system, so that the sun revolves around the earth and not the other way around. The three-tiered universe of the Old Testament and the Ptolemaic one of the New differ from one another significantly; however, both conceived of earth and humanity as the center of a much smaller physical creation.

Our modern scientific view of the world and our place in it has changed radically since the ancient authors composed the Bible. Not only do we acknowledge the earth is not the center of our solar system, but also our solar system is just a speck in one galaxy amongst thousands. We know, too, this universe where we are set is constantly expanding at an almost implausible rate. Furthermore, our understanding of human physiology, psychology, geology, history, medicine, and most other areas of knowledge have expanded such that they, too, are worlds apart from those of the Biblical authors. To impose their scientific worldview on us or vice versa requires dishonest intellectual compromises. But the Bible is not a textbook of any stripe, nor should we ever cheapen it by reading it as one. The Bible is a timeless library of books expressing the relationship of God to humanity. It chronicles the romance between God and us, and like all romances the story has had its ups and downs. Nevertheless, romances express what is most important and central to us. Therefore, it is not surprising it took early Christian leaders several hundred years to scrutinize what proposed writings really struck at the heart of our faith and should be permanently included in what we term the Holy Bible.

Heart matters are timeless, while the next scientific advancement is just over the hill. We will no sooner buy a new computer, cell phone, or camera before they are outdated. We will situate ourselves into the current cosmological paradigm with the uneasy realization that the chair will be pulled out from under us to make room for yet another advance. The message of the Bible, on the other hand, remains powerfully relevant and constant. That does not mean its message is static – far from it! All scripture is prophetic, meaning it continually speaks to each generation. Take the book of Job, for instance. Most of the epic poem likely predates Israel. The Jews adopted and edited the book with its prose prologue and epilogue because they realized it said something eternal about the human condition and our relationship with God. Prophecy works that way. First of all, the contents of Job were only shared orally for hundreds of years. To those earliest middle-eastern audiences of the book, who gathered at night around campfires in tribal bands to hear the lines recited by an elder or a traveling bard, the words illuminated the deep questions of their inner journey. Later, perhaps around the 1,000 BC in the court of David, Job was first written down by Hebrew scribes and no doubt edited in the process. The learned literate Jews would then share the wisdom of Job to illuminate their own generation. And when we read it in my little classroom in Western Maryland, the students and I glean many of the same lessons from the text and even stumble upon some new ones from time to time. Biblical prophecy works that way. It has a revealing word for every generation and culture where it is shared. Scripture remains prophetic; that is to say it states deep truths to every audience open to receive it.

Much of the Bible at first glance seems so tedious that we cannot imagine it to be wholly prophetic, which leads to the third rule of Bible reading: *Beware of cumbersome lists, impractical injunctions, and nonsensical stories in the scripture because there may be something important hiding in those lines.* What may seem dull, dated, and unusable may very well convey important prophetic truths. An example of this supposed tedium is the seventeen verses of genealogy at the beginning of the Gospel of Matthew. At first glance it seems like a patriarchal *Who's Who* written to mollify stuffy First Century male audiences of the Gospel. If we take a closer look at the genealogy, however, we find woven amongst the list five women – two seductresses, a prostitute, and an adulteress accompany Mary, the revered mother of Jesus. It must be noted that the four colorful women are added to the list because they rose above their circumstances and above the men with whom they associated to fulfill an essential part in God's purpose for humanity.[30] In a male-dominated ancient culture, Matthew begins his book with this veiled assertion that God uses unlikely people to further his work, and that means he will very likely use us, as unlikely and unworthy as we consider ourselves, if we remain open and obedient.

As for impractical injunctions, Jesus seemingly voiced his most unreasonable dictum on leadership more than once: *The last will be first and the first last.* (MT 20:16; 19:30; MK 10:31; LK 13:30) The quip dances off the tongue nicely, but seems highly unrealistic in our modern competitive age. You can bet it was just as impractical during the Roman Empire's martially enforced "global economy" as well. How interesting to note, however, in the militant economic times where we find ourselves that the bestselling business books of the past decade One Minute Manager, The Seven Habits of Highly Effective People, and Built to Last all hold up as examples of industry leaders and companies who pay almost sacrificial attention to the needs of their workers, customers and families – occasionally risking financial decline because of that demonstrated concern.

---

[30] Gail R. O'Day, David Peterson, eds., "Women in the Genealogy", The Access Bible (New York: Oxford, 1999), 4 (New Testament).

Covey writes in <u>The Seven Habits of Highly Effective People</u> that most conflicts we encounter at home and in the workplace can be resolved in a "Win-Win" solution. Another person does not have to fail in order for us or our company to advance. Yet to take the route to "Win-Win," a good leader must put himself aside to genuinely attend to another, perhaps someone with whom he fiercely disagrees or even dislikes. In Collin's and Porras's book, <u>Built to Last</u>, The Nordstrom Corporation is noted as having the best working environment and most customer satisfaction amongst all U.S. companies. Their management chart is an inverted pyramid with the president of the company at the bottom. He is listed in the most subordinate position on the chart to demonstrate that an effective leader's place is in support of his workers. The person who would be in first place must go to last. While I would not recommend justifying the entire contents of the Bible by its compatibility with commerce, it would be hard to render Jesus' injunction here as impractical in any age.

Of all the parables of the New Testament that infuriate my teenaged students, none rival the Parable of the Prodigal Son. Adolescents, with their keen sense of justice, find that most famous parable both unfair and senseless. In the story, a father had two sons. The younger son demands his share of the inheritance even before his father dies. The boy goes off to spend the money as fast as he can in bars and brothels, while the older son remains at home laboring daily on the family farm. When the younger son runs through the money, he begins to starve. So he takes a job with a pig farmer, where he spends his days craving the slop served to the pigs (Craving pork left-overs is quite a stretch for a Jew!). As his hunger grows, the young man realizes that his father's slaves receive better treatment than what he is experiencing from these strangers, so he sets off to beg for simple servitude – certainly not family status – back at the homestead. As the son nears home, his father recognizes his silhouette in the distance, causing the old man to pick up the hem of his robes, run out to the boy and embrace him. The boy tries to complete his much anticipated speech to apply for a slave's position, but his father will not let him finish. Instead, he orders his servants to remove the rags the boy is wearing and dress him in his father's most expensive robes, he takes the gold ring off of his finger and places it on his son's hand, and in a final spontaneous flair of affection, he declares a huge party shall be held for his missing son that very night.

Luke 15:20-24 (NRSV)

So he set off and went to his father. But while he was far off, his father saw him and was filled with compassion; he ran and put his arms around him and kissed him. The son then said to him, 'Father, I have sinned against heaven and before you; I am no longer worthy to be called your son.' But the father said to his slaves, 'Quickly, bring out a robe – the best one – and put it on him; put a ring on his finger and sandals on his feet. And get the fatted calf and kill it, and let us eat and celebrate; for this son of mine was dead and is alive again; he was lost and he is found!' And they began to celebrate.

If we imagine the younger son is astounded by his father's unexpected reception, consider the pent up ire of the older son. By the time the party is in full swing, his fury has hit crescendo levels. The older son not only refuses to attend the party, he won't even enter the house. The father goes outside to entreat his eldest son to come on in, but he is met by his son's stony response that although he has remained faithful, perhaps even having to double-up on farm chores since his brother's decadent foray, he has never even been offered a small party for his friends. Listening attentively, the father responds in appreciation for his oldest son's fidelity, but then urges him to put his rage aside and come in to a party for a brother they did not think they would ever see again.

Luke 15: 25-30 (NRSV)

Now the older son was in the field; and when he came and approached the house, he heard music and

dancing...Then he became angry and refused to go in. He
father came out and began to plead with him. But he
answered his father, 'Listen! For all these years I have
been working like a slave for you, and I have never
disobeyed your command; yet you have never given me
even a young goat so that I might celebrate with my
friends. But when this son of yours came back, who has
devoured your property with prostitutes, you killed that
fatted calf for him!'

My students side with the older brother all the way. Often one of
more of them will say, "I wouldn't go in to that party either! It doesn't
make sense that such a big deal should be made over a kid who
embarrassed you and left you holding the bag." Of course, Jesus was
hoping the story would at first strike its hearers as nonsense, too. He
wanted them to be shocked – even angered – and then humbled as they
realized how human mercy falls far short of God's. We are all Prodigal
Sons or Daughters, but our goal in Christ is to grow up gratefully into
someone resembling the father in the parable. When a story or
statement in the Bible seems utterly outlandish, we better read a little
more closely because it's likely to be a zinger we best not miss.

Luke 15: 31-32 (NRSV)

Then the father said to him, 'Son, you are always with me,
and all that is mine is yours. But we had to celebrate and
rejoice, because this brother of yours was dead and has come
to life; he was lost and has been found.'

People have been unfairly beat-up by some of the Bible's zingers,
too. Usually that occurs when a small portion of scripture is lifted from
the text in order to justify a particular viewpoint or group's position.
Therefore, the fourth rule of Bible reading is: *If you think a piece of*
scripture has been torn from a larger piece, it probably has. Remember the
Bible is a romance, and a single line of text reveals very little about the
fomenting love between two individuals in a human relationship. Can

you imagine taking the line, "Catherine fell breathlessly into the arms of Heathcliff" to describe the stormy love affair in Emily Bronte's <u>Wuthering Heights</u>? Of course not, the legendary Victorian saga is much deeper than that. The Bible is not comic strip material either. If all we were told from the story of the Prodigal Son was that his father raced out to greet his younger son or that the older son refused to enter the house, we would be missing the very sense of the story. Accordingly, the same is true if we just throw out John 3:16 to our friends or to the mass public on huge banners at televised athletic contests. *For God so loved the world that he gave his only begotten son to the end that all who believe in him may not perish but have everlasting life* is a wonderful truth and likely the most popular New Testament verse, yet it is fortified by the story of Nicodemus, a reluctant seeker, in which it is set. If we tear singular verses out of their narrative fabric, we are abbreviating God's prophetic message and perhaps dangerously wielding the words as our own. Again, we are all Nicodemus, the reluctant seeker, who puts on a confident front to cover up our great confusion. The thrust of Jesus' words to Nicodemus in John 3 is God's invitation to us, not his condemnation of us.

John 3: 16-17 (The Message)

'This is how much God loved the world: He gave his Son, his one and only Son. And this is why: so that no one need be destroyed; by believing in him, anyone can have a whole and lasting life. God did not go to all the trouble of sending his Son merely to point an accusing finger, telling the world how bad it is.'

How do I get started reading the Bible?

After noting the several pitfalls of Bible reading, it may seem daunting to crack open the big book you mainly connect with your grandmother's house, living room coffee tables, and dramatic waves across your television screen by big-haired evangelists. The hardest part of Bible reading, much like its indispensable partner prayer, is to crack open the book and begin. Thankfully, as we begin to read the Bible, we need not drag out commentaries, dictionaries, and sundry theological reference books. It is best to simply begin with a Bible and a quiet place in which to spend some quality minutes reading it.

For clear direction on a timeless Bible reading technique, I will return again to Benedictine monastic custom to employ their practice of *Lectio Divina* , meaning sacred study or reading, mentioned in the previous chapter. The steps in this ancient technique are simple. First, sit in a quiet, comfortable place, either alone or with a reading partner or two, and pray that the Holy Spirit will illuminate and inspire your reading. This first step is an acknowledgement that reading Holy Scripture is different from other routine reading because the words can be prophetic if we become open to the grace of them. We read the Bible to be changed on the inside, to be swept up in a romance with God. We should not read scripture to merely accumulate scriptural information bites.

The second step in *Lectio Divina* is to read the passage aloud two times. If you have a companion, you may take turns reading. Read slowly, so as to absorb each word. It is very important to read the Bible aloud. We do so because most parts of the Holy Scripture were shared aloud long before they were written down, and those that were first written, like Paul's letters, were composed to be read publicly. For our immediate purposes, however, it is important to both speak and hear the words, awakening both the senses of sight and sound.

After the second reading, choose a word or phrase that stands out for you in the reading. I have been amazed when I have done this with the same Bible story a second or third time. A different word or phrase leaps out to me from the page at most every reading. If I am honest, I will realize that I have moved to a new spiritual locale from the time before, and the scriptural prophecy has struck me in that different place. As an aside, I find it terribly boring and somewhat disturbing when a Christian gives the same testimony of an encounter with God year after year. It sounds as if they quit meeting with God after that singular epiphany. Serious engagement with the Bible will keep us from such stagnation.

Now, read the passage a third time. At the conclusion of that reading, sit for a moment and enter the scene described by the scripture. What do you hear, smell, and feel in that setting? Are you exhilarated, terrified, confused? The Bible is a living book like no other. We are not meant to hold it at arm's length. We should dare to enter the story and allow it to live inside of us. Any child will tell you that is the allure of the *Harry Potter* books and of C.S. Lewis's *Narnia Chronicles* before them. We can step inside the attic wardrobe and enter that wonderful and terrible land of Narnia or catch the magic train to *Hogwarts Castle*. In the same way, we can enter the Biblical narrative. We can step out from hiding amongst the crowd with David and confront Goliath, or let our heart almost beat out of our chest with Rahab as she hides some mysterious spies, or join reluctant Nicodemus as he sneaks at night to have a word with Jesus, or burn with both embarrassment and fury with Simon of Cyrene as the Roman cohort makes him carry the shameful cross for the condemned Jesus, or even break down in desperate sobs with Mary Magdalene as she begs the supposed gardener for Jesus' broken, lifeless body. We are meant to enter these stories, and not just occasionally – but everyday. If we have the courage to step into them, God will speak to us, and our faith will avoid corrosion.

Hebrews 4: 12-13 (NRSV)

Indeed, the word of God is living and active, sharper than any two-edged sword, piercing until it divides soul from spirit, joints from marrow; it is able to judge the thoughts and intentions of the heart. And before him no creature is hidden, but all are naked and laid bare to the eyes of the one to whom we must render an account.

In concluding our *Lectio Divina*, we read the Bible passage one more time. After this reading, we ask ourselves the painfully direct question: "What is God asking me to do?" Again, because Holy Scripture is prophetic, we are necessarily being asked to do something through the passage we have read now four times. Perhaps we have been David or his brothers cowering behind a rock wall of fear, yet now the scripture is calling us out to confront our enemy, likely the one on the inside, face-to-face. Maybe we are Mary Magdalene overcome with a loss with which we have never come to terms. We may even be Nicodemus, just skirting around the edges of our faith. The Bible is meant to bring us into the light of him who is the true abiding light.

I John 1:5-7 (NRSV)

This is the message we have heard from him and proclaim to you, that God is light and in him there is no darkness at all. If we say that we have fellowship with him while we are walking in darkness, we lie and do not know what is true, but if we walk in the light, as he himself is in the light, we have fellowship with one another, and the blood of Jesus his Son cleanses us from all sin.

In my office at home, there is a colorful painting that stares back at me from the mantel. It is an interpretation of an ancient mosaic at Ravenna depicting a very Roman Jesus as the Good Shepherd. The beautiful piece was a gift to me from a distinguished artist in my former congregation. Not only do I love to look at the painting as I am working, but the Biblical passage, John 10: 11-17 on which the painting is based, has long been the most convicting one in my life. With that admission, it suddenly occurs to me that I have never completed a *Lectio Divina* exercise using these verses, so I will do so today in order to illustrate this ancient reading technique.

John 10:11-17

'I am the good shepherd. The good shepherd lays down his life for the sheep. The hired hand, who is not the shepherd and does not own the sheep, sees the wolf coming and leaves the sheep and runs away – and the wolf snatches

them and scatters them. The hired hand runs because the
hired hand does not care for the sheep. I am the good
shepherd. I know my own and my own know me, just as
the Father knows me and I know the Father. And I lay
down my life for the sheep. I have other sheep that do not
belong to this fold. I must bring them also, and they will
listen to my voice. So there will be one flock, one
shepherd. For this reason the Father loves me, because I
lay down my life in order to take it up again.'

After reading the passage twice slowly, the phrase that leapt out to me is *who is not the shepherd and does not own the sheep* (v. 12). In all honesty, I tried to divert my attention to another passage, but this one hung onto my spirit. Likely, I wanted to avoid this particular phrase because of the two humble admissions I must make in the face of it: First, I must acknowledge that although I have been called "pastor" or "shepherd of the flock" many times, I am not the Good Shepherd. Only Jesus can fill that role, and that means that the "sheep" are his. No matter how many titles I gather for myself – *Father, Doctor, Reverend, Brother, Pastor, Minister* – the flock will never belong to me. The people filling any parish I serve, any classroom I teach, or any gym where I coach belong to Christ. I can only be Christ's steward of the sheep. Second, I often make a poor steward. These willy-nilly people about whom I often complain are precious to my Lord, and yet I cut and run from them more times than I would care to count. I often act like the *hireling...whose own the sheep are not.*

At the conclusion of my third reading of the scripture, I realize that I can insert myself into the passage two ways. I can put myself in that ancient pasture amongst all those bleating sheep or I can put myself in Jerusalem as Jesus confronts the adversarial Pharisees with this illustration. Either way, there is a wealth of sensory images that float through my mind. This time, however, I will enter the former scene in some lonely Judean hillside pasture. Perhaps I am showing my cynicism a bit, but the scene is far from idyllic. Because I live in farm country, often sharing my back yard with a couple dozen cattle, I sit amongst those sheep and smell the strong, sickly sweet aroma of manure, I hear sheep incessantly bleating to one another in complaint, and I see them rubbing their dirty woolen coats on me and on one another. On the other hand, due to my professional role, the sheep quickly become people gathering in a parish hall. The smell of manure is replaced by the scent of discarded coffee grounds, the sound of crowding sheep by the chatter of adult friends and scampering children, and the scene easily transposes from more sheep for whom you can adequately care to people you love but can't seem to love enough. The scripture has given me an avenue to feel and express my sense of pastoral inadequacy in the faces of the people drawn to the Church.

I read the passage for the final time and I ask myself the hard question, "What does God want me to do?" The first thing that hits me squarely between the eyes from this passage is that God wants me to quit running. My inadequacy is fueled by the fact that I sometimes imagine that I am the Good Shepherd and the care of all these people is mine. Those thoughts, of course, are idolatrous. Christ is God. The people are his. Christ is more than able to care for them and guide them to better pasture for their souls sake. I do not need to run because it is the Good Shepherd standing in the midst of the people, and I am one of those people. Also, I am running from the people because the major part of my work in the Church, like yours I imagine, is far from glamorous or even fun. The greater part of taking care of people is walking with them back to greener pasture, back to Christ. I would like to say the journey is always thrilling, but much of it is not.

I have a Bible that has traveled with me far more than any of my others. It is an unimpressive, 3x5", worn New Testament, with a shiny, fake leather, olive drab green cover. Yet I place it horizontally at eye-level on my shelves in front of my twenty or so stately study Bibles to remind me of the purpose and power of that book. I received that small New Testament on the first day of my Army enlistment and I took it with me through all my training, on every stateside exercise, and each overseas deployment. Usually, I would stuff it into one of my ammo pouches right in front of two 5.56 caliber ammunition banana clips. At other times, I squeezed it alongside my gas mask or medical kit. Regardless of how creative this infantryman had to be in order to find a place for this OD Bible, it made the trip. At night, sitting beside a newly dug foxhole or atop an APC (armored personnel carrier), I would unclip my red lens flashlight from my web-belt and pull the Bible from its hiding place, and read the lines of the gospels, letters, Revelation, and Acts. Inside the cover, I would write down verses that spoke to me the most powerfully at the time – verses illuminating the care of children, the *Great Commandment*, the resurrection, the light of Christ, prayer, forgiveness, the Kingdom of God, and the living water of the Holy Spirit.

Those verses I annotated twenty-five years ago still stir me in much the same way as Huck and Jim's muddy Mississippi flows somewhere deeply within me. They remind me that I am not an *accidental tourist* in this life. No, I am connected to something and Someone much larger and much more wonderful that I can fathom on this leg of the journey. In the introduction to his book <u>Walking the Bible</u>, Bruce Feiler writes about Abraham, the first personality of the Bible: "Abraham was not originally the man he became. He was not an Israelite, he was not a Jew. He was not even a believer in God – at least initially. He was a traveler, called by some voice not entirely clear that said: Go, head to this land, walk along this route, and trust what you will find."[31] Like our great-grandfather Abraham, we are not who we ought to be yet, but we are on our way.

[31] Bruce Feiler, <u>Walking the Bible: A Journey by Land Through the Five Books of Moses</u> (New York: Harper Collins, 2001), 3.

Discussion Questions for Chapter 7
Why Read the Bible?

Our Stories

Recall the last time you were really moved by a good novel, biography, or movie? What elements in it touched you and why?

Reading Review

1. How is the Bible an adventure book?

2. Why is Bible reading more fun if you know what you are reading?

3. In what way can we become like our great-grandfather Abraham through reading the Bible?

Bible Connections

1. Read **Hebrews 4:12-13**. What do these lines about the Word (Jesus) tell us about God's ability to powerfully communicate with us?

2. Read **Luke 4:1-13** and the study notes that accompany it? How important was the Bible for Jesus during this fearful encounter?

3. Read **Luke 4:16-21** and the study notes that accompany it. How does Jesus use the Bible *prophetically* on this occasion?

4. Read **Luke 9:46-48**. Study this passage using the ancient tenets of *Lection Divina*. How do the words come alive for you through this process?

Chapter 8

What's All the Fuss about Eternal Life?

What's the point of eternal life?

I stood at the intersection of the Gulf Highway and Moss Point Road for two hours before I conceded I was forgotten. It was the summer of my junior year in High School, and my family had just moved from Birmingham, Alabama to Pascagoula, Mississippi, a small industrial city on the southern gulf coast. The occasion for the move was my mother's marriage to a big, friendly construction worker, and while I was pleased that she finally had a companion, I was worried about remaining friendless the entire summer. Those fears were allayed, however, one Friday afternoon in mid-June. A girl I met from a church we had visited on Sunday kindly invited me to a pool party she was hosting the following Friday. I felt out of place for the longest time at the big gathering until three guys my age struck up a conversation with me at poolside covering the trinity of concerns most central to every teenaged boy – football, cars, and girls. An hour or so into our exchange, they asked if I would like to go camping with them over the weekend on a part of the beach they particularly liked. I jumped at the opportunity. We exchanged phone numbers, I received the proper permission from my mother, I put together a duffle bag full of the items they prescribed for the trip, and then I walked to the appointed crossroads. My three new friends were to pick me up at 8:00 PM in a red GTO. After one hour had passed, I figured there had been some hold up, so I walked the half mile back to my house to see if they had called. No one had. I returned to the crossroads and looked eagerly at every red Pontiac that passed. Finally, at 10:00 PM I slung my duffle bag over my shoulder and slowly headed home. When I stepped heavily into the hall, my mother uttered sleepily from her bed, "Pat, are you sure they weren't just playing a trick on you?" The words struck me hard in the gut.

I never found out the real story because I did not see those boys again, and after that summer we moved back to Birmingham. But I do remember how humiliated and hurt I felt. Being forgotten is painful stuff. As a matter of fact, I think our fear of abandonment is our deepest and most persistent terror. Just think of the toddler who is left with a sitter for the first time, remember your first night at summer camp, recall that first week on a military deployment, or the death of parent or grandparent. At those times, we have felt a sickening mix of loneliness and betrayal deep in our guts. Fears of abandonment haunt us more than anything else.

When I was completing my infantry officer training, I recall the scrupulous instruction we received on what to do if taken prisoner-of-war. At one point during these sessions, we were introduced to another officer who told us how he survived four years in a North Vietnam prison. Beginning that day, the thought of being apprehended by some terrorist group operative in my unit's region of deployment along the East German border terrified me. Being forgotten by my unit, my government, and eventually forgotten even by my family appeared worse to me than death. Like you, I bet, I remain somewhat the toddler who fears losing sight of his loved ones more than anything else.

However, continued fear of abandonment can retard our growth as persons. Afraid that we will be forgotten and discarded by others, we process through life with the creed "do not trust, do not feel, and do not love." We become like the *Michelin* tire man, buffeted from contact on all sides. Better to insulate ourselves than risk the shock of rejection. Remember Miss Havisham, the pitiful recluse in <u>Great Expectations</u>, who is forsaken by her fiancée on their wedding day? She, in turn, imprisons herself in her home, leaving the wedding cake, gifts, and lacey decorations to rot all around her until her own death. The author, Charles Dickens, is painting his readers a revolting picture of how a life decays if frozen with the fear of loss. The suffocating fear of abandonment that incarcerates and corrodes a person can only be dispelled by that perfect love and fidelity expressed in the life of Jesus. In fact, Jesus considered his main task from God was to gather us to himself for eternity and assure us he would do so.

John 6: 37-39 (NRSV)

Everything that the Father gives me will come to me, and anyone who comes to me I will never drive away; for I have come down from heaven not to do my own will, but the will of him who sent me. And this is the will of him who sent me, that I should lose nothing of all that he has given me, but raise it up on the last day.

As surprising as it may seem, however, two stories in the New Testament tell of people who fearfully imagined Jesus had not only forgotten them, but left them for dead. Jairus, the leader of a local Galilean synagogue, feared Jesus had forgotten his family during their darkest hour. He had begged Jesus to hurry to his home so he could heal his dying daughter, yet Jesus was held up by the pressing needs of those crowding about him at another place. When Jesus finally arrives, the cries of those attending the dead child turn to laughter at him, feebly masking their anger and hurt over his late arrival.

Mark 5:38-42 (NRSV)

When they came to the house of the leader of the synagogue, he saw a commotion, people weeping and wailing loudly. When he had entered, he said to them, 'Why do you make a commotion and weep? The child is not dead but sleeping.' And they laughed at him. Then he put them all outside, and he took the child's father and mother and those who were with him, and went in where the child was. He took her by the hand and said to her,

*'Talitha cum,' which means, 'Little girl, get up!' And
immediately she got up and began to walk about.*

The most powerful accusation that Jesus had abandoned those
whom he loved was uttered by the sisters Mary and Martha, Jesus'
dear friends whom I introduced in Chapter 6. The two sent Jesus word that
their brother Lazarus was quite ill, hoping Jesus would hurry to them
and restore their brother's health. Again, as in the story of Jairus's
daughter, Jesus is delayed so long in his arrival that Lazarus dies. In fact,
by the time Jesus makes it to their home in Bethany, Lazarus has been
in the tomb several days and the air is rife with the wails of family,
friends, and professional mourners. As Jesus approaches the house,
Martha rushes out to greet him and the resulting encounter is one of
the most moving in the entire New Testament.

John 11: 17-26 (NRSV)

*When Jesus arrived, he found that Lazarus had already
been in the tomb four days. Now Bethany was near
Jerusalem, some two miles away, and many of the Jews
had come to Martha and Mary to console them about
their brother. When Martha heard that Jesus was
coming, she went and met him, while Mary stayed at
home. Martha said to Jesus, 'Lord, if you had been here,
my brother would not have died. But even now I know
that God will give you whatever you ask of him.' Jesus
said to her, 'Your brother will rise again.' Martha said to
him, 'I know that he will rise again in the resurrection on
the last day.' Jesus said to her, 'I am the resurrection and
the life. Those who believe in me, even though they die,
will live, and everyone who lives and believes in me will
never die.'*

The drama of the story intensifies when Jesus asks to be taken to
the cave tomb where Lazarus has been buried. It is one of the most

graphic miracle scenes in the Bible, and Martha's persistent resistance to Jesus adds to the tension of the account.

John 11: 38-44 (NRSV)

Then Jesus, again greatly disturbed, came to the tomb. It was a cave, and a stone was lying against it. Jesus said, 'Take away the stone.' Martha, the sister of the dead man, said to him, 'Lord, already there is a stench because he has been dead for four days.' Jesus said to her, 'Did I not tell you that if you believed, you would see the glory of God?' So they took away the stone. And Jesus looked upward and said, "Father, I thank you for having heard me. I knew that you always hear me, but I have said this for the sake of the crowd standing near, so that they may believe that you sent me.' When he had said this, he cried with a loud voice, 'Lazarus, come out!' The dead man came out, his hands and feet bound with strips of cloth, and his face wrapped in a cloth. Jesus, said to them, 'Unbind him, and let him go.'

When it looks to all concerned that Jesus is too late to save their loved ones, they discover instead that he is right on time. In both of these stories, as the people's fears explode at Jesus in jabs of anger, ridicule, and doubt, he goes to the deceased and then personally leads them out of death. When Jesus says to Martha, "I am the resurrection," he is claiming eternal life is bound up in his intimate relationship with each one of us. The resurrection is not mechanical, as if God sits back and pushes the "up" button for us to ride the divine elevator. On the contrary, the resurrection is personal. The very good news is Jesus so dearly loves us that he will never leave us at the crossroads of life and death.

Because eternal life is irrevocably tied to Jesus' communion with us, the resurrection can only be clearly understood if seen through the light of the crucifixion. Jesus doggedly marches through derision and torture to a humiliating death on a cross out of love for us, and he who marches out in front of us to Calvary is the same Lord who will lead us from death to eternal life. Our destiny is permanently enmeshed with his. We are traveling with him on the same road leading from death into life. This certainty is powerfully stated by our Lord in his final conversation on the cross:

Luke 23:39-43 (NRSV)

One of the criminals who were hanged there kept deriding him saying, 'Are you not the Messiah? Save yourself and us!' But the other rebuked him, saying, 'Do you not fear God, since you are under the same sentence of condemnation? And we indeed have been condemned justly, for we are getting what we deserve for our deeds, but this man has done nothing wrong.' Then he said, 'Jesus, remember me when you come into your kingdom.' He replied, 'Truly I tell you, today you will be with me in Paradise.'

On this accord, I have caught myself telling countless individuals and groups, "It is Christ's faithfulness not our own that makes him savior." Our entire Christian hope is built upon Jesus' faithfulness to us and not the other way around. If we are honest, we know we have much in common with the criminals hanging on each side of Jesus. We deserve to die. As much as we may candy-coat our lives in our own imaginations, each one of us has failed to live up to the holiness prescribed by God that is beautifully manifested on earth by Jesus. Ironically, Christ's death –the death of the most beautiful – provides the escape from our own sinfulness.

However, like the criminals crucified beside Jesus, his sacrifice for us is only half the story. The resurrection is the other half. "Jesus, remember me when you come into your kingdom," we say in the hope that a love so great to die for us will also be strong enough to save us from death. Yet most of us are somewhat like Martha that day mourning over the death of her dear brother Lazarus. The resurrection has arrived and is standing right in front of her, but she does not yet see him. As we come to believe in Jesus and fully trust his love for us, the resurrection will become more and more a present and continuing reality to us. The One who wonderfully created us and then astonishingly bears our sins to Calvary can be counted upon to draw us eternally into unity with himself. The cross and the empty tomb stand as the two pillars of God's unfailing remembrance of us. St. Paul passionately expressed this great hope of Jesus' unrelenting fidelity to us by connecting his love expressed in crucifixion with the resurrection:

Romans 8:31-39 (NRSV)

> *If God is for us, who is against us? He who did not withhold his own Son, but gave him up for all of us, will he not with him also give us everything else? Who will bring charges against God's elect? It is God who justifies. Who is to condemn? It is Christ Jesus, who died, yes, who was raised, who is at the right hand of God, who indeed intercedes for us. Who will separate us from the love of Christ? Will hardship, or distress, or persecution, or famine, or sword...No, in all these things we are more than conquerors through him who loved us. For I am convinced that neither death, nor life, nor angels, nor rulers, nor things present, nor things to come, nor powers, nor height, nor depth, nor anything else in all creation, will be able to separate us from the love of God in Christ Jesus our Lord.*

What is eternal life?

If we are confident that God will never forget us, what then is the substance of eternal life? The idea of the resuscitation of our corpse after physical death is not appealing. Most would agree that our bodies are "out of warranty" by middle age. Accordingly, the dualist notion that we have detachable souls which live on while our body is discarded is an abstract notion discounting the integration of what makes us whole persons. Neither of these two notions, while widely ascribed, are scriptural. In order to get our arms around the nature of eternal life, we should first look at St.

John's biblical reports surrounding Jesus own resurrection. Mary Magdalene does not recognize the risen Jesus until he speaks her name (John 20:16). Thomas will not believe Jesus has walked out of the stone hewn tomb until he sees the holes in his body made by the nails and sword (John 20:27). John and Peter do not know the resurrected Jesus is speaking to them from the bank of the Sea of Galilee until he directs them to a huge catch of fish (John 21:6). During that first Easter week, Jesus is not immediately recognizable by those who knew and loved him, and yet essentially he is the same. When they look harder, Jesus closest friends realize the resurrected Jesus is the one they knew before he was executed at Calvary. St. Paul does not dispel all the mystery surrounding our inheritance of eternal life, but he does offer a vision of our resurrection consistent with Christ's own defeat of death:

1 Corinthians 15:50-55 (The Message)

I need to emphasize, friends, that our natural, eartlhy lives don't in themselves lead us by their very nature into the kingdom of God. Their very 'nature' is to die, so how could they wind up in the Life Kingdom? But let me tell you something wonderful, a mystery I'll probably never fully understand. We're not all going to die – but we are all going to be changed. You hear a blast to end all blasts from a trumpet, and in the time you look up and blink your eyes – it's over. On signal from the trumpet in heaven, the dead will be up and out of their graves, beyond the reach of death, never to die again. At the same moment and the same way, we'll all be changed. In the resurrection scheme of things, this has to happen: everything perishable taken off the shelves and replaced by the imperishable, this mortal replaced by the immortal. Then the saying will come true:

> *Death swallowed by triumphant life!*
> *Who got the last word, oh, Death?*
> *Oh, Death, who's afraid of you now?*

Like, Jesus, our forerunner into eternal life, our decaying bodies will be changed, yet we will essentially be the same person in the resurrection. In other words, the "Pat" I am now will be the same "Pat" in heaven. Following my Lord, my appearance may be changed, but the core of what makes me – me will be unchanged. Pat, then, will always be remembered by God. Noted Cambridge physicist John Polkinghorne gives the most plausible modern explanation of our transformation into eternal life that strongly echoes Paul's ancient understanding:

> The pattern that is me will be dissolved at death. Death is, therefore, a real end, but it is not the ultimate end, for only God is ultimate. It is a perfectly coherent belief that the pattern that is me will be remembered by God, held in the mind of the faithful Creator, and that God will ultimately reconstitute through the divine, eschatological act of the resurrection into a new environment. In other words, my soul will be reembodied when I am raised to the everlasting life of the world to come. The ultimate act of the resurrection will not involve the matter of this present creation. Paul was right to say that "flesh and blood cannot inherit the kingdom of God, nor does the perishable inherit the imperishable" (1 Corinthians 15:50). If it did, resurrection would only mean being made alive again in order to die again. Our destiny is something altogether more hopeful than that. [32]

Occasionally, I will exclaim to my youngest son after one of his spontaneous comical monologues, "John, they broke the mold when they made you!" Lately, he has begun to retort, "Dad, they broke the mold when they made each one of us!" Our banter reveals a profound theological truth – there is only one divine pattern that is you, one that is me, and one that

---

[32] John Polkinghorne, "Opening Windows onto Reality," Theology Today 58 (2001): 145-154.

is each person of every color, location, and age on this planet. Each personal pattern continues forever in the memory of God.

It is important to note here that Jesus is our only Biblical example of eternal life. While the resurrection of Jairus' daughter and Lazarus are magnificent miracles, both persons underwent another physical death at some point. Furthermore, modern near-death accounts are intriguing and often inspiring, but, again, we have no modern exemplar of a resurrected person. Humans are limited by the boundaries of temporal time; therefore, our experience of eternity will be when we are in the middle of it. From the Greek, eternal time – God's time – is termed *kairos*. Such time escapes the linear boundaries of the clock. Occasionally in our earthly lives, we have caught glimpses of *kairos* when we played *hide-n-go-seek* in the backyard on a summer's night, spent the afternoon with a sweetheart, experienced the births of our children, kept watch at the bedside of a sick friend, took a walk in a primeval forest, or were swept away by the beauty of Sunday morning worship. On those magical occasions, the second hand on the clock cannot control time. It is as if time bends. Madeline L'Engle's much loved science fiction book, <u>A Wrinkle in Time</u>, describes this experience through the contrasting eyes of both adult scientists and children, demonstrating our life-long ability to slip into small slices of eternity.

Jesus and the disciples walk into a short passage of *kairos* when they ascend Mount Tabor. Arising from a short nap after the climb, the disciples awake to find Jesus "transfigured" into a radiant heavenly appearance and speaking with both Elijah and Moses. The disciples are so moved by the experience that they ask if they can build some booths there so they can reenter *kairos* at will (Matthew 17, Mark 9, Luke 9). Their request could not be fulfilled. *Kairos*, like grace, is a gift from God, and we cannot will ourselves into it anymore than we can will our own salvation. Thus, sometime later when the disciples meet the resurrected Jesus, he now fully inhabits *kairos*, while they are still firmly "on the clock." For that reason, Jesus appears essentially the same, but they cannot quite get their arms around him.

This complete transformation from temporal to *kairos* time also will happen to us. Time will, in fact, lose its power over us. The moment by moment decay of our bodies and the press and rush of ultimately unimportant things will cease. Two important conclusions can be drawn from this fact. For one, it will make no difference to us whether we inherit eternity in the immediate way promised to the criminal crucified next to Jesus, or if we enter eternal life on some great last day the way Paul describes in 1 Corinthians 15. Either way, we will have escaped the prison of temporality. Second, our entrance into eternal life can commence immediately. As we give ourselves more and more to God, the grasp of time and all its seductive minions gradually will lose their grasp on us, and God will be faithful to lead us deeper into *kairos*. We will discover that we were ultimately made for that leap.

When does eternal life begin?

I have been led into *kairos* occasionally. Admittedly, I spent more time there as a child than I have as an adult. I have been swept away for much of my adult life by things that don't matter eternally, and I have felt Jesus calling me back to the grace I once felt so clearly when I was younger. When he says, "Whoever does not enter the kingdom of God as a little child, will never enter it," he is not just throwing out a semantic ditty (Mark 10:15). The faith of a child that draws him or her into the timeless, unbounded love of God's domain is the most palpable foretaste a person will have of eternal life.

For my part, I cannot contemplate those childhood forays into heaven without thinking of the Flynns. All through my tough adolescent years, the Flynn family from our Birmingham neighborhood took me on vacation with them each summer. Their oldest son Danny and I played sports together at the local public park. The Flynns were not wealthy people by any stretch of the imagination. In fact, that first summer they mentioned the trip to me, my mother told me that I must have been mistaken. She was afraid she was catching the idle conversation of two thirteen year-old boys and she did not want her own son hurt. However, just a day or two latter, Betty Flynn, Danny's mother, showed up at our door to formally issue the invitation. I do not think I missed a single summer vacation with that gracious family during my teenaged years.

What made my vacations with the Flynns so wonderful was my immediate incorporation into their family. Never once did I feel like a "fifth wheel." I remember so well that Mr. Flynn would buy a huge tube of fresh salami from the butcher, white bread, mustard, and the cheapest soft drinks at the grocery store. All of us kids would play hard all morning, feast on that fare in the afternoon, take a luxurious mid-day nap on the bunks in our crowded lakeside cabin, and then start all over again. Those summer days seemed to stretch out forever. For me, it was like a sojourn in Eden, surrounded by the three Flynn children, their parents, and other friends. That faithful, gracious, working-class family helped me overcome my abundant adolescent fears of inadequacy and abandonment by my father, just by the simple act of remembering me. They ushered me into *kairos* time, and my imagination of those endless days has directed my adult path when I have let it.

A conversation I shared with Mr. Flynn on my second or third vacation with his family further illustrates the transforming influence they have had in my life. Everyone was still asleep when I awoke and found Mr. Flynn sitting outside, drinking his coffee, and reading his paper. Much like my own father, he was a big, freckled, barrel-chested, Irishman. I really loved Mr. Flynn, and I felt his great affection for me. After I sat with him that morning for 30 minutes or so, I said, "I wish my dad was like you. Then he wouldn't have left us." Mr. Flynn put his paper down and looked hard at me. "Pat, you had better let go of your anger toward your father. You don't know his whole story." He then matter-of –factly brought the paper back up to his face signaling that was as much as he had to say on that matter. I never forgot what he said, though. A major reason for my strong emotional health as a young adult was that I heeded Mr. Flynn's words and gave up the anger and fear surrounding my father's absence. It did not happen all at once. My father exited our lives when I was ten years old, the oldest of his four children. He only reentered our lives four or five more times during our childhoods, and he paid only one payment of $50 in child support during all those years. So, I had a great deal of pain to get over – especially as I watched my mother struggle and my siblings doing without. But Mr. Flynn's prophetic words that early morning at lakeside continued to convict me. I forgave my father and was able to accept him as a severely wounded veteran from the Korean Conflict who never healed himself. At the core of my forgiveness of him was my belief that he really did not forget us children; rather, he was just too beaten up himself to reach out to us. This one act of forgiveness unshackled the procession of my adult life from childhood regret. In the months leading up to my father's early agonizing death from liver cirrhosis, I was able not only to completely forgive him but to love him as I did when a very young boy.

To consider our particular pattern abiding forever in God, as Dr. Polkinghorne describes, may be disconcerting. I mean, we must begin by examining just what kind of pattern we have already become. Given the magical mix of carbon dust and genetic wiring that makes each person on this planet distinctive, how have we expressed or failed to express the beauty of our particular divinely ordered pattern? In short, what is expected of the Christian who awaits the resurrection? What have we done with what we have been given? Again, we should look to Jesus for the answer and the example we need.

Only St. Luke tells the post-resurrection story often termed "the Emmaus Walk." Later on that first Easter Sunday, two of Jesus' followers are making their way out of Jerusalem, both terribly despondent and disillusioned that Jesus had been executed and with his death their hopes for God's redemption of Israel. As they meander along, Jesus joins them, but they do not recognize him due to his resurrected guise. Along the way, Jesus interprets the scriptures for them so that they begin to see the hand of God at work in the events leading up to and culminating at Golgotha. The two are so enrapt and encouraged by their unexpected companion's wisdom they beg him to remain with them for supper and rest. During the meal, the stranger breaks the bread and their eyes are opened to see it is unmistakably Jesus in their company. He may not look the same, but the wonderful things he said and did were the same pattern of the man they had come to know, love, and follow during his three earthly years of ministry. It was a great surprise that the one they saw brutally crucified was now sitting with them at supper, but the grace he exuded in his words and actions led them to positively recognize the Jesus they had known in temporal time.

Luke 24: 30-32

When he was at the table with them, he took bread,
blessed and broke it, and gave it to them. Then their
eyes were opened, and they recognized him; and he
vanished from their sight. They said to each other,
'Were not our hearts burning within us while he was
talking to us on the road, while he was opening the
scriptures to us?' That same hour they got up and
returned to Jerusalem; and they found the eleven and
their companions gathered together.

Jesus' witness to us in this vignette from Luke is that life in the resurrection, eternal life, is a dynamic existence. The unique genetic pattern that is you and the one that is me and the unique path of growth each of us undertakes in this earthly life are a prelude to the promised life to come. We Christians are not fatalists. We do believe each one of us is a unique creation with distinctive gifts and challenges, but we do not believe that we are torpid beings incapable of growth. In other words, we are not just "the hand we have been dealt." If we are willing, God intends to continually enhance the patterns that are us, making us more like Christ and drawing us ever closer to him.

This eternal transformation of our life in Christ is very much on my mind as I write these lines. Just yesterday, my mother called to tell me that my Uncle Joe had died. He had been in a fight with cancer for some time, and finally the illness prevailed. Yet Joe was far from sickly during his trials. In fact, he seemed to grow more robust in spirit with each bad medical report. During the past year, when my mother suffered the losses of both her husband and her youngest son, it was Joe who extended himself to her in his steady, unassuming, and most unselfish way. Very much like Jesus healing the spirits of those two downcast disciples on the Emmaus Road, Joe turned a light on for Mother, and all the while he was swiftly falling into death himself. Undoubtedly, that is the key to unlocking the resurrected life. Once we gather up enough courage and honesty to admit to ourselves we are dying, and we all are, of course, the door opens for us to give ourselves away unreservedly. "To lose our lives" is the essential mark of Christly growth because we begin to see clearly the utter absurdity of trying to "save" ourselves (Matthew 10:39; 16:25; Mark 8:35; Luke 9:24).

Of all the things he did in his last months that amazed me, Joe's purchase of a huge RV was the most astounding. How could he possibly imagine he and my Aunt Kathy were going to travel very far from the reach of the hospital and his considerable medical care? Where did he think he was going? Now, I know he was certain of his destination and the behemoth RV was just a symbol, a sacrament of sorts to the rest of us, to mark the journey he had undertaken. Submitting his earthly life to Christ, Joe began traveling into eternity. Uncle Joe's enormous RV should remind us all, too, that this is a trek for which all Christians should prepare. In our own life's journey, just as in the life of Christ, our resurrection is irrevocably yoked to our personal crucifixion.

Romans 6:5-11 (NRSV)

For if we have been united with him in a death like his, we will certainly be united with him in a resurrection like his. We know that our old self was crucified with him so that the body of sin might be destroyed, and we might no longer be enslaved to sin. For whoever has died is free from sin. For if we have died with Christ, we believe we will also live with him. We know that Christ being raised from the dead, will never die again; death no longer has dominion

over him. The death he died for sin, once for all; but the
life he lives, he lives to God. So you must also consider
yourselves dead to sin and alive to God in Christ Jesus.

Eternal life is a journey that embarks the moment we give ourselves fully into God's hands and trust him to transform us. He is the one who composed the patterns that is each one of us, and through the power of the Holy Spirit we can grow forever more into the person we were fashioned to be. Lest we imagine we are in the "driver's-seat" of our growth, a dear friend of mine tells me each time we meet, "In the beginning God, and in the end God." We are conceived by God and transformed by God so that we may eternally abide in God. We are God's doing and our growth into the resurrection is his doing. St. Augustine was somewhat stunned that people questioned the power of God to refashion us for the resurrection. The miracle of our birth, he states, is a preamble to the miracle that marks our second birth.

People are amazed that God, who made all things from nothing, makes a heavenly body from human flesh. When he was in the flesh, did not the Lord make wine from water? Is anything much more wonderful if he makes a heavenly body from human flesh? ... Is he who was able to make you when you did not exist not able to make over what you once were?[33]

Looking at eternal life from this angle, it is not surprising that Mr. Flynn's curt advice to me so many years ago comes to my mind. The resurrected life is one directed away from one dead-ended in regret and fear. Preparing for eternity is not to rein back life but to push the throttle wide open, letting go of those things which once loomed important in our lives but now seem inconsequential. We are, as Augustine asserts, to undergo a "make-over." Anger, revenge, timidity, rage, envy, lust, – all those things drift away like Dandelion seeds when

---

[33] Augustine, <u>Sermons for the Feast of the Ascension</u> 264.6, cited by Gerald Bray, <u>1-2 Corinthians: Ancient Christian Commentary on Scripture</u> (Downers Grove, IL: Inter Varsity Press, 1999), 182.

viewed through eternity. How utterly paradoxical – if we loosen our grip on this transitory, earthly life that is coming to an end the very moment we take our first breath, we may begin the resurrected life that parades forever into the heart of God. Why wait?

Colossians 3:1-4 (The Message)

So if you are serious about living this new resurrection life with Christ, act like it. Pursue things over which Christ presides. Don't shuffle along, eyes to the ground, absorbed with the things right in front of you. Look up, and be alert to what is going on around Christ – that's where the action is. See things from his perspective.

Discussion Questions for Chapter 8
What's All the Fuss about Eternal Life?

Our Stories

Recall an occasion when you felt forgotten or ignored. Describe as specifically as possible the pain you endured at that time.

Reading Review

1. Why must *eternal life* be seen "through the light of the crucifixion"?

2. Who will you be in the resurrection?

3. When does eternal life begin, and what does "kairos" have to do with it?

Bible Connections

1. Read **John 6:37-39** and **Luke 23:39-43**. Should we fear Jesus Christ forgetting us?

2. Read **Luke 24:13-35**. Why was the resurrected Jesus not initially recognized by the two men? What opened their eyes to Jesus' true identity? Do you see a connection here between Jesus' resurrected self and what we will be in the resurrection?

3. Read **Romans 6:5-11**. According to Paul, how do we participate in Christ's crucifixion and our resurrection?

4. Read **Revelation 21:1-8**. According to John of the Revelation, what is God's plan for the earth in the resurrection? How should that affect our reverence for our world today? On the other hand, what is Jesus' warning about the 'second death"?